Meeting Environmental Challenges: The Role of Human Identity

Meeting Environmental Challenges: The Role of Human Identity

Tom Crompton and Tim Kasser

First published in 2009
by WWF-UK
Panda House, Godalming,
Surrey, GU7 1XR
www.wwf.org.uk

© WWF-UK

Distributed by Green Books Ltd.
Foxhole, Dartington, Totnes,
Devon TQ9 6EB
www.greenbooks.co.uk

ISBN 978-1-900322-64-5

WWF's Strategies for Change Project

This publication is one of a series produced as part of WWF-UK's Strategies for Change Project. This project seeks to examine the empirical basis for today's dominant approaches to environmental communications and campaigns, and to ask why these are failing to create the level of change that is needed. Electronic versions of this book, and other related publications, can be freely downloaded at: **www.wwf.org.uk/strategiesforchange**.

Join the debate!

We hope that this short book will stimulate wide and critical debate – not just amongst the environmental movement, but amongst the third sector more generally. To help support this debate, we have set up a website, **www. identitycampaigning.org**, which we will use for developing these ideas further, testing them, and inviting critical comment.

FOREWORD

Crisis can bring opportunity. It challenges the institutions that guide our decision-making and it can profoundly affect our individual sense of identity. The growing worldwide awareness and experience of economic, social, and environmental crises seem to be prompting a renewed confidence among people to ask fundamental questions: Where are self-enhancing and materialistic values leading us? How important is our relationship to people on the other side of the world and to other species? What needs to change if we are to cope with the overwhelming scale of the problems humanity faces?

We cannot know with any certainty where such questioning will lead us. But this publication, *Meeting Environmental Challenges: The Role of Human Identity*, helps clarify how the environment movement and the third sector as a whole can begin to respond to these challenges. The authors have amassed a sophisticated theoretical and empirical case for a fundamental re-evaluation of mainstream approaches to environmental communications and campaigning. Their thinking goes beyond an analysis of the problems of our current approach: it also suggests clear and intriguing new possibilities that hold a great deal of promise.

Agree with it or challenge it – but either way, prepare for change.

David Norman
Director of Campaigns
WWF-UK

CONTENTS

INTRODUCTION

The epochal scale of today's environmental challenges is now beyond serious scientific dispute. Awareness of the scale of these challenges grows ever greater – in the case of climate change, it seems that the prognoses of climatologists grow yet more urgent on an almost weekly basis. And as this awareness grows, so too does our understanding of the gulf between what needs to be done and what is actually being done.

The environmental movement has achieved a great deal in attempting to meet these environmental challenges, investing remarkable effort with limited funding against powerful countervailing forces. In these attempts, the environmental movement pursues two basic types of strategy: engaging *organisations* (both government and businesses) and engaging the particular *behaviours* that individual citizens pursue. Here we present an overview of these two strategies as a prelude to introducing a third approach to which we feel the environmental movement must pay close attention. We believe that this third approach, which we call *identity campaigning*, holds substantial promise for enhancing the effectiveness of the movement's current work and for developing useful strategies for new types of intervention.

Engaging organisations

Much of the environmental movement's current focus is on engaging organisations. For example, one dominant approach relies upon the development and refinement of policy proposals, coupled with political lobbying to encourage the adoption of these proposals by government. This is an important strategy; there is no doubt that the environmental movement has been pivotal in the development of many key environmental policy proposals, and in successful political campaigns to see these adopted by government. Consider, for example, the development of new efficiency standards, restrictions on pollution, or the establishment of protected areas.

But, as most environment campaigners would probably agree, current policy responses fall far short of the level of intervention needed, and this approach is frequently vulnerable to the critique, levelled by Shellenberger and Nordhaus in their paper *The Death of Environmentalism*, that "[t]he environmental movement's technical policy orientation has created a kind of myopia:

everyone is looking for short-term policy pay-off" (Shellenberger and Nord-haus, 2003: 25).

Interrelated constraints imposed by a lack of political leadership and a lack of electoral demand – along with opposition from strong vested interests – often frustrate attempts to create policy interventions, so that these do not deliver the extent of regulatory change needed to address systemic environmental problems.

In failing to respond properly to today's environmental challenges, governments are guilty of capitulating their leadership responsibility – and the lack of public pressure for ambitious new government interventions cannot excuse this failure. Nonetheless, in the face of this regrettable government timidity, it is crucial that environmental organisations find more effective ways to generate and mobilise public pressure for change. How will irresistible electoral demand for sufficient regulatory intervention and global leadership emerge? Today's environmental movement doesn't seem to have a clear response to this question.

Responding to the problem that business interests often present for policy reform, a second, more conciliatory approach to organisational engagement seeks to demonstrate a convergence between commercial interest and environmental imperative – the 'business case for sustainable development'. There is no doubt that where this convergence can be found (for example in improvements in the efficiency of the use of raw materials or energy in a production process), environmental impact can be reduced at the same time that money can be saved (or made). The prospect of better leveraging this coincidence of commercial and environmental interests has led to the frequent insistence by government that environmental challenges be met through 'de-coupling' economic growth and environmental impact. Such approaches place emphasis, for example, upon opportunities to dismantle market distortions (including subsidies, or tariffs on trade in environmental goods and services) that both exacerbate environmental problems and depart from today's neo-liberal economic orthodoxy. Clearly, making such cases can be environmentally beneficial, and is often politically expedient.

Important as these interventions are, emphasis upon the economic prudence of some environmental measures risks fuelling a reluctance to confront other policy interventions that may not lie so comfortably with the grain of current economic orthodoxy. Such cases arise frequently. Environmental regulation is often opposed on the grounds that it will conflict with economic growth, and such claims sometimes bear scrutiny – particularly where a short-term perspective is taken, or high discounting rates are assumed. More often still, ambitious regulatory interventions may never even be publicly discussed because of the *chilling*[1] effect of insistence that environmental regulation must be compatible with economic growth, the profits of businesses, or the sovereignty of consumer choice.

In sum, a focus on engagement with organisations – whether government or private sector – can point to clear successes in driving through new environmental policies and regulations, and changes in business practice. But such interventions are proving woefully inadequate. If they are to be made proportionate to the scale of challenge we face, this will likely be as a result of both new and bold government and business leadership, and of public pressure.

Engaging behaviour

The second dominant approach, of engaging specific behaviours, is typified by presenting individual citizens with checklists of 'things you can do to reduce your ecological footprint'. By focusing on behaviours, the political difficulties inherent in engaging organisations are avoided and emphasis is shifted away from government and business onto the individual. Increasingly, approaches to motivating behaviour change retreat from using information campaigns coupled with moral exhortations; this is certainly understandable, given the limitations of such strategies. Instead, approaches to motivating the uptake of particular behaviours typically draw on marketing techniques. The emphasis of such campaigns is upon motivating large numbers of people to adopt specific behaviours – often to make 'simple and painless' choices. These techniques offer obvious opportunities to collaborate with manufacturers and retailers to urge new forms of 'green consumerism', and are thus complementary to the organisational strategies described above. Such approaches to engaging behaviour usually remain indifferent about the deeper values or goals that motivate people to adopt these behaviours; campaigns might, for example, appeal to the financial savings that accrue from switching to low-energy light bulbs or fitting double glazing, or the status that comes with purchasing a hybrid car or a bottle of organically grown wine. Focus is maintained on the behaviour, rather than the people engaging in the behaviour. To the extent that the people and their motivations are considered, this is with a view to better tailoring communications to urge a change in behaviour – it is not with a view to examining and shifting underlying values or goals.[2]

Certainly this approach makes perfect tactical sense in creating piecemeal behaviour change, and it no doubt works well for marketing agencies contracted to sell as many units of a particular product as possible. Behaviour also has the advantage of being easily examined and analysed – an action is performed, or it is not. But campaigns focused primarily on simple and painless behaviour changes may well work against the emergence of a set of goals and motivations that will lead to more systemic adoption of pro-environmental behavioural choices. What's more, experimental evidence does not support the common assumption that, having adopted one specific pro-environmental behaviour, people are then necessarily more likely to engage in other more difficult and significant pro-environmental behaviours (WWF, 2009).

Identity campaigning

Both of the dominant approaches outlined above – focussing on organisations and on behaviours – can point to important successes. But it is also clear that neither has generated the political space and irresistible pressure necessary for adequate regulatory intervention, the fundamental reform of business practice, or the far-reaching changes in individual lifestyle choices that will be needed in order to meet today's environmental challenges.

Given the enormity of these challenges and the inadequacy of current strategies to meet them, we have attempted in this short book to delineate a third type of approach to environmental campaigning that the environmental movement has thus far seemed largely to neglect. We call this identity campaigning, as it focuses on those aspects of a person's identity that either lead them to demand more ambitious change on the part of organisations, or that underlie their motivation to engage in pro-environmental behaviour. Our proposal is that acquiring an understanding of the psychological make-up of the person who participates in organisations and who makes private-sphere behavioural choices, will help both of the dominant approaches to be more effective. Further, identity campaigning will help environmental organisations to foresee and avoid some of the ways in which current strategies may have counter-productive effects. Finally, understanding the psychological make-up of the person opens up a number of additional types of interventions that can be used in efforts to address environmental problems.

To this end, we suggest that there are certain aspects of the human psyche that create proclivities towards unsustainable behaviour. In this book, we focus on three specific aspects of human identity. We will argue that these proclivities are often reinforced, or enabled, by social norms and structures, by the government policies that shape these, and even sometimes by the actions of environmental organisations themselves. It seems to us that today's environmentalism by and large either retreats from confronting these aspects of identity, choosing to ignore them, or alternatively attempts to 'work with' them, trying to co-opt them to serve environmental purposes. Unfortunately, as we shall see, co-opting them risks making these environmentally problematic aspects of identity even more prevalent.

It is important to emphasise that we are not suggesting there is anything abnormal about these aspects of identity – quite the opposite. These are ubiquitous facets of the human psyche. They may be just as basic to the psyche of those who strive to minimise their environmental impact as they are in those who are indifferent to such impact. But their ubiquity does not mean that these facets of human nature are necessarily dominant, or that other, competing and more positive aspects of identity cannot be brought to the fore.

It is inevitable that our society, however structured, will serve to make some aspects of human identity more prevalent than others. It is also clear that governments play a key role in this process. Policy makers may be "uncomfortable with the idea that they have a role in influencing people's values and aspirations. But the truth is that governments intervene constantly in the social context" (Jackson, 2009: 94). Our interest is in the ways that social context serves to accentuate those aspects of identity which, according to the research we present, tend to undermine approaches to meeting environmental challenges.

It seems to us that the mainstream environmental movement has rarely invested resources into examining these environmentally problematic aspects of human identity, identifying the social structures that enable and accentuate them, and working to change these structures so as to encourage more environmentally beneficial aspects of human identity. And yet, until an understanding of the person is integrated with current environmental strategies, and until the environmental movement begins to tackle these aspects of identity and the social norms and structures that enable them, we fear that responses to the environmental crisis will remain inadequate.

The first step in this process, of course, is to examine more publicly how certain aspects of human identity are associated with environmental problems; Part I of this book begins this process. The second step is to identify strategies to mitigate the extent to which these aspects of human identity are encouraged, and to promote alternative aspects that are not so damaging; Part II of this book undertakes that examination and proposes a number of new approaches, strategies, and perspectives on environmental campaigning. Finally, in Part III we highlight some of the opportunities that this approach to environmental campaigning offers, and the grounds for optimism that it can be of crucial importance in supplementing, modifying, or replacing current campaign strategies. In particular, we develop a case for extending identity campaigning to address concerns and challenges beyond environmentalism, and point to the opportunities for new and concerted approaches to joint campaigning across a diverse range of third-sector organisations.

PART I:
HUMAN IDENTITY AND
ENVIRONMENTAL CHALLENGES

In Part I we identify three aspects of human identity that empirical research suggests are associated with behavioural decisions that often serve to frustrate optimal responses to environmental challenges. *Identity* refers to people's sense of themselves: who they think of themselves as being. Most identity theorists agree that identity influences how people respond to the broader social world and how they choose to live their lives, and that this sense of self emerges from the confluence of internal psychological dynamics on the one hand and the social context on the other.

Clearly there is substantial room for subjectivity in deciding which aspects of the human psyche in general, and of human identity in particular, are especially important in determining humans' responses to environmental challenges. Our choice of the processes described below is based on three main factors. First, of course, is our own particular knowledge of psychology. Second, as alluded to above, is the existence of theoretical and empirical work demonstrating that these aspects of human identity are associated with unsustainable responses to environmental challenges. Third, as will be seen in Part II, is the existence of evidence suggesting that these aspects of identity might be amenable to a variety of interventions.

We make no claim that the three aspects of identity we have selected constitute a complete list, or that we have even succeeded in identifying the most important features of the human psyche involved in frustrating the emergence of proportional responses to environmental problems. Rather, our hope is that this analysis will stimulate those in the environmental movement to further examine the ways in which their communications and campaigns influence aspects of identity, so that existing strategies for promoting sustainability will be made more effective, and so that new strategies can be developed.

Chapter 1

Values and life goals

Values and life goals are the aspects of people's identities that reflect what they deem to be desirable, important, and worthy of striving for in their lives (Rokeach, 1973; Schwartz, 1992)[3]. As with other aspects of identity, values and goals have both internal determinants, based on psychological needs and drives, and external determinants, based on the social models and experiences people encounter (Schwartz, 1992; Kasser, 2002). Substantial empirical and theoretical work demonstrates that values and life goals have important ramifications for people's attitudes and behaviours (Feather, 1992). This is because values and life goals are understood to be higher-order cognitions that influence the more specific attitudes individuals hold with regard to the people, objects and ideas they encounter in the world. For example, compared to someone who cares little about security, a person who believes security is important is likely to be more attracted to home security systems, and to be more supportive of governmental policies that ensure low crime rates – even if these come at the cost of some civil liberties. Values and life goals are also understood to reflect higher-order motivations that organise the more specific goals and low-level *behaviours* that constitute many aspects of people's day-to-day lives (Emmons, 1989). So, for example, security values are likely to influence whether a person holds the handrail while descending steps or which of several different investment opportunities he or she will pursue.

Substantial cross-cultural research has identified around a dozen values and goals that consistently emerge across nations. What's more, as we shall see later, the organisation of these life goals and values is remarkably consistent across cultures.

Among these is a set of values and goals focused on wealth, rewards, achievement and status. For example, Shalom Schwartz and colleagues (1992, 2006) have identified the existence of two types of *self-enhancing* values that consistently emerge across 70 nations as fundamental and coherent aspects of people's value systems. Schwartz calls these values 'power', or the desire to dominate people and resources, and 'achievement', or the desire to demonstrate one's success relative to others.[4] Other work by Grouzet and colleagues (2005) across fifteen nations has documented the cross-cultural emergence of a similar set of life goals, labelled *extrinsic* or *materialistic*. These goals, which are focused on the attainment of external rewards and social praise, include specific aspirations for financial success, popularity and having a socially desirable image.

Quantitative empirical studies document that people who strongly endorse such self-enhancing, materialistic values also express more negative attitudes towards non-human nature. For example, Wesley Schultz and colleagues (2005) studied almost 1,000 university students from six nations and found that values for power and achievement were associated with viewing humans as consumers of, rather than part of, nature. Schultz and colleagues also reported that stronger values placed on power and achievement are associated with less concern about how environmental damage affects other humans, children, future generations and non-human life. Where these self-enhancing values promote concern about ecological damage, this concern is limited to an egotistic consideration of how such damage might affect one *personally*. Similar results in Australia (Saunders and Munro, 2000) and the US (Good, 2007) have been documented for measures related to materialistic goals: caring more about such goals is associated with significantly less positive attitudes towards the environment, and with lower levels of biophilia (the desire to affiliate with life).

Values have been found to influence behaviour as well as attitudes. Studies in the US and the UK show that adolescents who more strongly endorse materialistic goals in life report themselves as being less likely to turn off lights in unused rooms, to recycle, to reuse paper and to engage in other positive environmental behaviours (Gatersleben *et al.*, 2008; Kasser, 2005). Similar findings have been reported for American adults, amongst whom materialistic values are found to be negatively correlated with the frequency of engagement in pro-environmental behaviours such as riding a bicycle, reusing paper, buying second-hand, and recycling (Brown & Kasser, 2005; Richins & Dawson, 1992). Brown & Kasser (2005) also examined how the ecological footprints of 400 North American adults were associated with their goals in life. A relatively high focus on materialistic goals related to a higher ecological footprint arising from lifestyle choices regarding transportation, housing and diet.

Game theory research further supports these results. Kennon Sheldon and Holly McGregor (2000) assessed college students' value orientation before asking them to play a forest-management game in which they simulated directorship of a timber company. Each subject (or timber company) then made a series of bids against three other companies to harvest wood from a state forest. Sheldon and McGregor arranged the groups so that they were either composed of four subjects who all scored relatively high in materialistic goals, of four subjects who all scored relatively low in these goals, or of a mix of high and low scorers. The experiment then proceeded as follows: each subject made an initial bid for harvesting timber, the total of the four bids was subtracted from the existing forest acreage, 10% of the total remaining acreage was added back to represent re-growth in the forest, and the next year of bidding commenced. This process continued either until 25 years had passed or until no forest remained. Sheldon & McGregor found that in comparison to other groups, those composed of four individuals who all scored relatively highly in materialistic goals exploited the forest resources more intensively, and were significantly less likely to have any trees remaining at the 25th year of bidding.

Finally, data at the national level also demonstrates negative associations between environmental behaviour and materialistic values. Kasser (in press, a) correlated archival data about the values of large samples of undergraduates and teachers in 20 wealthy nations with the amount of CO_2 each nation emitted in 2003. As expected, even after controlling for gross domestic product (GDP), per capita CO_2 emissions were higher in countries where citizens placed a greater priority on pursuing goals such as wealth, achievement and status.

In sum, to the extent people prioritise values and goals such as achievement, money, power, status and image, they tend to hold more negative attitudes towards the environment, are less likely to engage in positive environmental behaviours, and are more likely to use natural resources unsustainably.

Chapter 2

In-groups and out-groups

Another defining feature of a person's identity is his or her *social identity*, or the groups to which that person feels he or she belongs. When people ask the question "Who am I?" they typically answer by including their membership of particular groups based on gender, race, nationality, profession, religion or political leanings, as well as their membership of smaller groups such as being fans of certain football teams or types of music (Tajfel & Turner, 1986). When a person encounters other individuals who share the same social identity, those others are considered part of the person's *in-group*. Recognition of potential members of the in-group holds many benefits, including the sense of belonging so important to humans.

While identifying oneself through membership of a group provides some important psychological benefits, it also has a cost: the classification of others into an in-group seems to automatically create an *out-group* comprised of those who differ in a particular aspect of identity. An extensive body of social psychological research on social identity demonstrates that after having classified others as belonging either to the in-group or to the out-group, people typically treat members of these groups in ways that enhance the standing of their in-group relative to the out-group (Hewstone *et al.*, 2002; Whitley & Kite, 2006).

In-group and out-group categorisation forms the basis of many psychologists' understanding of the widespread phenomena of stereotyping, prejudice and discrimination. That is, people's in-group identifications can lead them to believe that people who differ from them in ethnicity, race, age or sex are less unique, intelligent, moral or worthy of benevolent treatment than people who are "the same as me".

The idea of social identity has been extended to include a person's sense of belonging to nature. Drawing on work studying values and pro-environmental behaviour, social and behavioural scientists have introduced the concept of *environmental identity*. Clayton (2003) defines environmental identity as:

> A sense of connection to some part of the non-human natural environment, based on history, emotional attachment, and/or similarity, that affects the ways in which we perceive and act toward the world... An environmental identity can be similar to another collective identity (such as a national or ethnic identity) in providing us with a sense of connection... and with a recognition of similarity between ourselves and others. (p.45-46)

In recent years, a number of studies have begun to examine pro-environmental behaviour and environmental attitudes from an identity framework (Bragg, 1996; Clayton, 2003; Hirsh & Dolderman, 2007; Kals *et al.*, 1999; Light, 2000; Neisser, 1995; Reist, 2004; Schultz, 2002; Zavestoski, 2003). The examination of *self-construal* and the construct of *connectedness with nature* (Schultz, 2002) is of particular interest. Such connectedness refers to the degree to which an individual associates self with nature (Dutcher *et al.*, 2007), and it is understood as arising as a result of an individual's beliefs about the extent to which he or she is part of the natural environment (Arnocky *et al.*, 2007). Individuals who feel that they are part of nature have views of nature and self that overlap significantly; conversely, individuals who feel that they are not part of nature have views of nature and self that do not overlap.

Authors interested in environmental identity argue that experiences of environmental identity are important in developing a relationship with the natural world and that, in turn, a relationship with the natural world fosters pro-environmental behaviours. Schultz (2000), for example, suggests that:

> Environmental concern is tied to a person's notion of self and the degree to which people define themselves as independent, interdependent with other people, or interdependent with all living things. From this perspective, concern for environmental issues is an extension of the interconnectedness between two people. (p.394)

Much as with aspects of social identity, an environmental identity offers a sense of association and belonging to a group. So, to the extent that people consider themselves part of nature, or see nature as part of their in-group, we would anticipate that they will be more likely to act in pro-environmental ways. But to the extent that they see themselves as separate from nature, it is expected that they are more likely to behave towards it in damaging or exploitative ways.

Studies of environmental identity and connectedness with nature have indeed established that connectedness is strongly correlated with environmental attitudes and behaviours (Frantz *et al.*, 2005; Mayer & Frantz, 2004; Schultz, 2001). For example, in a large cross-cultural study of residents in 14 countries, connectedness with nature emerged as one of the strongest and most consistent motivational predictors of pro-environmental behaviour (Schultz, 2001).

The tendency to define humans as an in-group is called *anthropocentrism*. This is a consequence of a perceived split between humans and non-human nature, and we suggest that it leads to a heightened indifference to the suffering of both individual non-human animals and the destruction of the non-human natural world (including other species and ecosystems). Human attitudes towards other animals offer a particularly clear example of the human tendency to display prejudice towards non-human nature as an out-group.

Several empirical studies have examined the proposition that non-human animals constitute a type of out-group (Plous, 2002). For example, following a long-established tradition for studying how people categorise human personality types, Gerard Saucier (2003) asked experimental subjects to rate themselves, someone they liked or someone they disliked on a series of English (American) language nouns that can be used to describe people. Saucier then used a statistical procedure called factor analysis to understand how people's descriptions of others were organised in their minds. These analyses yielded evidence for a single, underlying dimension reflecting the extent to which a person is socially acceptable or unacceptable. While animal nouns were not strongly associated with words conveying social acceptability, a remarkable number of the nouns used to describe socially unacceptable people were animal words (for example, 'weasel', 'dog' or 'pest'). These findings suggested to Saucier that "describing an individual in nonhuman terms implies that the individual is 'not one of us', that is, he or she should not be a *bona fide* member of one's own human group" (p.707). The use of animal nouns in a derogatory way, to deprecate human out-groups, also belies a prejudice against animals as an out-group themselves.

Other studies similarly show the tendency to associate out-groups with animals. For example, Jacques-Philippe Leyens and colleagues (2001) noted that most people believe that both humans and animals experience "primary emotions" (like joy, anger, surprise and fear) but that only humans experience "secondary emotions" (like remorse, affection, pride and conceit). Subjects in several studies reported that members of their in-group are more likely to experience these uniquely human, secondary emotions than are members of the out-group. Fundamentally then, people denied out-group members some level of *humanness* by presuming that they shared a lower level of emotional development, comparable to that of non-human animals.

Additional research has extended these findings by showing that this process of *infrahumanisation* occurs for characteristics besides emotions. For example, Viki and colleagues (2006) presented British study participants with common British names or with names typical of other languages, and with lists of words typically associated with humans (e.g. wife, civilian) or with animals (e.g. wildlife, creature). Using a variety of different methods across four studies, Viki found that British participants were significantly more likely to associate human words with British names than with foreign names, and significantly more likely to associate animal words with foreign names than with British names.

So it seems that humans tend to associate out-group humans with animals as a way to justify prejudice towards human out-group members. This probably reveals a tendency to treat animals as an out-group themselves: something that helps to explain widespread human indifference to the mistreatment of animals. (As illustration of this, think about when playground insults liken members of a different gang to people who are mentally disabled; this reveals a prejudice not just towards members of that other gang, but also towards disabled people). This, in turn, seems to be one facet of an anthropocentric perspective that helps to explain humans' high level of tolerance for the destruction of non-human nature.

Evidence for this perspective is found both in historical studies and reports of empirical investigations. In a historical study of changes in attitudes towards the natural world in England between 1500 and 1800, Thomas (1983) concluded that the ways in which people justify dominating other animals are an inherent aspect of humanity's broader attempt to dominate the natural world. In an experimental study, Vining (2003) found that those who ascribe greater rights to individual animals also express more positive orientations toward the environment.

In sum, we suggest that there is a continuum between indifference to the suffering of individual animals and indifference to the loss of entire species or destruction of ecosystems, and that both these attitudes are driven in part by a tendency to see non-human nature as the ultimate out-group. The tendency to define non-human nature as an out-group will frustrate the emergence of a stronger connection to nature, and thus undermine the likelihood that people will engage in more pro-environmental behaviour.

Chapter 3

Coping with fear and threats

The third aspect of human identity that we highlight concerns how humans attempt to manage threats to their existence, their self-esteem and the integrity of their identity. Such threats often create emotions such as anxiety, guilt and existential angst, which are not only unpleasant to experience in their own right, but can also interfere with people's capacity to function normally. As such, people use a variety of strategies to attempt to cope with such threats. Sigmund Freud (1923/1961) and his daughter Anna Freud (1936) first identified these as *defence mechanisms*, defining them as mental operations used (often unconsciously) by individuals to manage such threats. Since Freud's time, substantial empirical evidence has clearly demonstrated that a range of such mechanisms are commonly used by humans in response to feelings of anxiety and guilt, threats to one's self-esteem and identity (Baumeister, *et al.*, 1998; Cramer, 1991), and reminders of one's own death (Greenberg *et al.*, 2000). Researchers from other perspectives have also discussed similar psychological processes that serve essentially the same functions, referring to these as *coping strategies* (Lazarus, 1991; Zeidner & Endler, 1996), *therapeutic strategies* (Stoll-Kleemann *et al.*, 2001) or *emotional management strategies* (Hochschild, 1979). Regardless of their name, this body of literature shows that people have at their disposal an extensive array of psychological strategies to help them suppress thoughts and feelings about anxiety-producing situations and to protect their identity.

There seems little doubt that awareness of the scale of environmental problems that humans confront can lead people to experience a sense of threat. For example, people are likely to feel scared and anxious when confronted with scientists' projections about natural disaster, disease, war and food shortage. Anxiety, guilt (a kind of moral anxiety) and threats to self-esteem can also result when people recognise their own complicity in exacerbating these environmental problems. Threats to existing identity probably also arise when people realise that they will have to fundamentally change many aspects of their lives either in order to avert ecological catastrophe, or to cope with catastrophes once these occur.

Although some anxiety-producing situations can be escaped physically (one can run away from a dangerous confrontation or leave an abusive relationship), in the case of environmental crisis, this is not possible. The impossibility of physical escape from environmental problems propels some people to adopt radical changes in the way that they live (in order to minimise their own environmental impact), or to engage in direct political action. But for all those who have engaged in such environmentally beneficial means of coping, there are many others who apparently attempt to deal with awareness of ecological crises through psychological strategies that do not promote such beneficial ecological outcomes. In the next five sections, we provide an overview of a range of such defence mechanisms, coping strategies, or emotional management strategies. In each case, theoretical or empirical studies suggest, firstly, that people use these strategies to minimise the anxiety specifically associated with ecological problems, and to protect their existing identities; and, secondly, that these strategies do not promote positive environmental behaviour and often lead to negative environmental behaviour.

3.1 Strategies for diversion

One type of defence mechanism or coping strategy that people sometimes use when confronted with environmental problems involves attempting to supplant the anxiety-arousing information with other material. Kari Norgaard (2006) calls these "selective attention" emotion-management strategies. In her extensive ethnographic study of small-town Norwegians, she identified three ways that people distracted themselves when thoughts of global warming created feelings of fear or helplessness.

First, her respondents would *limit their exposure* to information which may create anxiety. For example, one environmental activist described how she avoided reading all of the details about global warming, believing that it is "better not to know everything". This may also manifest itself as a reluctance to engage in conversation about climate change. George Marshall refers to this as the 'Spinach Tart effect', reporting someone's experience at a dinner party: there was an awkward pause in conversation after a guest raised the issue of climate change, until another intervened by remarking on how lovely the tart was – at which point everyone else emphatically agreed (Marshall, 2007). Another form of selective attention involved *keeping one's thoughts in the present*, so that awareness about future impacts of climate change is avoided. For example, a young mother said, "There is a lot that is negative. Then I become like — yeah, pfff! … and so it is well that I don't allow myself to think so far ahead." A third type of selective attention Norgaard identified was *doing something*, however small. In work conducted with focus groups in Switzerland, Stoll-Kleemann and colleagues (2001) also identified this strategy, labelling it the "metaphor of displaced commitment". By turning down the thermostat a few degrees, or turning off the water whilst brushing their teeth, people can at least temporarily displace their feeling of hopelessness by taking action.

Homburg and colleagues (2007) suggest another diversion strategy that should be listed alongside those that both Norgaard and Stoll-Kleemann and colleagues identified: *seeking pleasure*, or deciding to pursue exciting experiences or possessions despite environmental problems. In the words of a recent advertising campaign for a new television channel in the UK: "Enjoy some glamour and gratuitous sex before the world ends."[5] In their study of eight different strategies that people use to cope with environmental problems, Homburg and colleagues found that 'seeking pleasure' was the strategy most highly endorsed across three samples of adults. Perhaps people's tendency to use the seeking-pleasure strategy so extensively was due in part to the fact that it seemed to provide psychic relief from anxiety. Indeed, Homburg and colleagues found a negative association between the extent to which people reported using this strategy and the level of stress they reported as arising from an awareness of environmental problems. Unfortunately, additional analyses showed that seeking pleasure did not motivate positive environmental behaviours, and in some samples this strategy was actually associated with less engagement in such beneficial behaviours.

3.2 Strategies for reinterpreting the threat

A second common set of strategies that researchers have identified seeks to diminish the unpleasant emotions arising from environmental damage by re-interpreting the situation so as to render it less threatening – particularly in terms of the challenge that it poses to one's sense of being a good person.

For instance, Homburg and colleagues (2007) studied the coping strategy of *relativisation*, which entails claiming that the ecological problems facing humanity are really not so great, or at least are smaller than other challenges that humans have successfully faced in the past. As with seeking pleasure, Homburg and colleagues found that this strategy was consistently associated with lower levels of stress from environmental damage, suggesting that it does reduce anxiety. However, as with seeking pleasure, analyses showed that endorsing relativisation did not promote greater pro-environmental behaviour.

Another reinterpretative strategy, *denial of guilt*, yielded similar results. When deploying this strategy, people coped with environmental problems by claiming that environmental damage is "not my fault". Again, as with other strategies we have discussed, denial of guilt helps lower levels of stress from environmental problems but did not propel people to engage in positive environmental behaviours. Stoll-Kleemann and colleagues reported the same strategy amongst their Swiss focus groups, with one respondent saying: "I alone can do nothing, I can achieve something only if the others join in" (2001: 113). Norgaard (2006) found similar results in her study of Norwegians, noting the frequency with which her respondents explained away their complicity in climate change by saying how globally insignificant Norway was – both in terms of cumulative national greenhouse gas emissions and international political influence.

A third reinterpretative strategy is the classic Freudian defence mechanism of *projection*, in which one's own feelings of guilt are denied and instead other individuals or groups are identified as the ones to blame. Norgaard found substantial evidence for this form of emotion management, as many of her Norwegian respondents repeatedly identified "Amerika" as the real source of ecological problems. Similarly, a Swiss focus group member said, "As long as the USA don't do anything…" (sic) (Stoll-Kleemann *et al.*, 2001: 113).

3.3 Strategies for indifference

Another class of strategy for coping with the fears and anxieties brought about by environmental degradation is *apathy*. Public apathy about the environment is often discussed in the environmental movement, and activists typically attribute apathy to insufficient information, information that is improperly presented, lazy citizens, or self-enhancing and materialistic values. Renée Lertzman (2008) has recently suggested an alternative way of understanding apathy: perhaps it represents individuals' attempts to protect themselves from the psychic pain they would otherwise experience if they accepted the facts about what they see as a hopeless, impossible situation. Psychotherapists have long recognised that if one believes that there is no hope, a good way to protect oneself is to seem not to care: if the problem is not personally important, it poses less of a threat.

Unfortunately, of course, apathy serves to reinforce behavioural choices that exacerbate environmental problems. Indeed, Homburg and colleagues found that people were significantly less likely to engage in pro-environmental behaviours to the extent that they used the strategy of *resignation*, accepting environmental problems as inevitable.

3.4 Orienting towards materialistic goals

A fourth common strategy for self-protection in the face of threat is to activate valued elements of one's identity and to strive to demonstrate that one is a worthy person. The theoretical perspective known as terror management theory (Solomon *et al.*, 1991), for instance, has repeatedly and empirically documented that when briefly reminded of the threat of their own mortality, people seek out means of enhancing their self-esteem (see Greenberg *et al.*, 2004).

In Chapter 1 we reviewed evidence that self-enhancing, materialistic goals are fundamental strivings present in most people's value systems. Given the current economic and cultural climate that frequently serves to equate an individual's worth with his or her financial status and possessions, it seems probable that, when briefly reminded of their mortality, people will tend to orient towards self-enhancing, materialistic values. A growing body of evidence suggests that this is the case.

For example, two recent studies showed that subjects randomly assigned to write short essays about their own death attached greater importance to money, image and status than other subjects randomly assigned to write about a neutral topic (Kosloff & Greenberg, 2009; Sheldon & Kasser, 2008). In another research project, subjects who had written about their own death reported being more excited at the prospect of finding $20 while out for a walk than those who had written about a neutral topic (Solomon & Arndt, 1993). Mandel & Heine (1999) also found that thinking about death (as opposed to about depression) increases the appeal of high-status goods. Specifically, after having mortality made salient, subjects were more attracted to goods such as a Lexus car or a Rolex watch, whereas thinking about death did not increase the appeal of a Geo-Metro car (a small and efficient vehicle) or Pringles potato chips. Writing about their own death has also been found to increase undergraduates' expectations about their future financial worth, as well as how much they expect to spend on clothing, entertainment and leisure activities (Kasser & Sheldon, 2000).

These studies suggest that *brief* thoughts of one's own death can increase the appeal of materialistic values, with the unfortunate ecological consequences noted in Chapter 1.

3.5 Denigrate the out-group

As we have just seen, one way people cope with threat is to activate valued parts of their identities. One important aspect of many people's identities concerns their in-group memberships (see Chapter 2). Thus, it is perhaps not surprising that threat is one of the key features that tends to promote in-group bias and out-group prejudice (Stephan & Stephan, 2000). What's more, the specific threat that occurs when contemplating one's own death has been shown to have the same effect: thinking about death leads judges to assign harsher punishments to prostitutes, Americans to provide greater monetary rewards to those who uphold common cultural values, and college students to be more antagonistic towards out-group members (see Greenberg *et al.*, 2004). These basic strategies for managing awareness of one's own death have been documented in several different cultures and for in-group/out-group differences based on religion, nationality, and political beliefs, as well as a variety of other outcomes.

On the basis of evidence reviewed in Chapter 2, we might expect that when people identify themselves in distinction to non-human nature, they will become especially negative towards animals and the natural world when reminded of their own death. Research suggests that this is indeed the case.

In the first test of these ideas, Jamie Goldenberg and colleagues (2001) conducted two experiments in which college undergraduates wrote essays either about their own death or about a neutral topic. In the first experiment, subjects then completed a survey assessing how disgusting they found several topics. Results showed that subjects who had written about their own death became especially disgusted by animals (seeing maggots or cockroaches) and body products (aspects of humans' existence that we share with animals, such as vomit or faeces). In the second experiment, after writing about death (or, in the case of the control group, about a neutral topic), subjects read essays emphasising either the similarities or the differences between humans and animals. The similarity essay read, in part:

> The boundary between humans and animals is not as great as most people think ... what appears to be the result of complex thought and free will is really just the result of our biological programming and simple learning experiences.

The differences essay read, in part:

> Although we humans have some things in common with other animals, human beings are truly unique ... we are not simple selfish creatures driven by hunger and lust, but complex individuals with a will of our own, capable of making choices, and creating our own destinies. (Goldenberg et al. 2001: 432)

When asked to evaluate the authors of these essays, the subjects who had written about the neutral topic expressed essentially the same attitudes towards both authors. In contrast, the subjects who had written about their own death rated the author of the essay proclaiming the similarities between animals and humans as less likable, intelligent, and knowledgeable than the author who wrote that humans were unique and special. Since these studies were conducted, additional research has similarly demonstrated that thoughts of death can cause people to express more negative attitudes towards those aspects of human behaviour that are shared with animals, such as breastfeeding and the physical aspects of sex (Goldenberg *et al.*, 2006), and towards animals in general (Beatson & Halloran, 2007).

Consistent with our suggestion that antipathy to non-human animals is a particular instance of antipathy towards non-human nature (see Chapter 2), these effects of mortality awareness extend to attitudes towards nature and wilderness. As Sander Koole and Agnes Van den Berg (2004) have noted, while many humans find nature and wilderness to be a source of awe and inspiration, people also often associate nature and wilderness with fear and terror. Indeed, Koole and Van den Berg found that subjects were significantly more likely to report that they thought about death when they were in wild nature (nature which humans have hardly affected) than when they were in either cultivated nature (meadows or grain fields) or the city (downtown or on highways). Reminders of death, compared to a neutral topic, were also found by these researchers to cause subjects to view cultivated, humanised nature as more beautiful and to rate wild, untamed nature as less beautiful. It seems, then, that thoughts of death lead many individuals to become more appreciative of a safe, tamed landscape (where humans have had extensive influence on the environment) and to become more negative towards wilderness.

If awareness of people's inevitable death leads them to respond more antagonistically towards wild nature, then it might also stimulate a tendency to transform or even destroy wilderness. Tim Kasser and Kennon Sheldon (2000) presented data supporting this possibility, based on an experiment in which subjects participated in a shorter version of the forest-management game described earlier (see Chapter 1). After writing brief essays about their own death or about listening to music, subjects were requested to imagine that they were in charge of a timber company, and were asked to make bids as to how many acres of trees in a state forest they would like to cut down. Subjects who had written about death made bids to cut down significantly more acres of forest.

3.6 Summary

In summary, threats can lead individuals to engage a variety of strategies to reduce unpleasant emotions and to retain high levels of self-esteem and identity integrity. Many such strategies exist, but some of them do little to promote positive environmental behaviour and can actually increase the likelihood of engaging in destructive environmental behaviour.

PART II:
IDENTITY CAMPAIGNING: STRATEGIES FOR ADDRESSING THE ENVIRONMENTALLY PROBLEMATIC ASPECTS OF HUMAN IDENTITY

Having established the environmentally problematic influence of self-enhancing, materialistic values, of in-group identities that separate humans from nature, and of the environmentally maladaptive strategies that people sometimes use to cope with threats and fears, we turn now to suggestions for interventions. As we shall show in the next three chapters, a focus on human identity can not only help environmental organisations refine existing campaigns, but can also point to the possibility of deploying a range of strategies that are at present largely overlooked by the environmental movement.

Chapters 4, 5 and 6 present a variety of strategies for interventions concerning self-enhancing, materialistic values, out-group prejudice, and defence and coping mechanisms, respectively. We begin each chapter by laying out a basic strategy for engaging each environmentally problematic aspect of identity. Although these basic strategies are specific to each aspect of identity, some elements of a common strategy also emerge. It is worth drawing attention to three such elements at the outset.

The first common element concerns elimination of *iatrogenic effects*. In medicine, iatrogenic effects are adverse conditions that are inadvertently induced by the activity of a doctor – that is, the patient becomes sicker as a result of the treatment. There is no doubt that the campaign activities of environmental organisations can be highly effective in creating specific policy changes or motivating particular pro-environmental behaviours. Nonetheless, some of the campaign tactics commonly deployed by the environmental movement may inadvertently serve to reinforce the environmentally problematic aspects of identity that we identified in Part I. Such campaigns, therefore, may *exacerbate* environmental problems in the longer term because they promote those very features of human identity that contribute to environmental degradation. In the chapters that follow, we will provide examples of such iatrogenic effects and suggest means of addressing them and replacing them with more effective strategies.

Clearly, our main reason for drawing attention to these effects is in the hope that they might be better managed. But there is another important reason for this self-scrutiny. As we have emphasised elsewhere, the aspects of identity that we have highlighted in this report are ubiquitous. Environmentalists certainly do not transcend them – either as consumers, as members of a group who define themselves in distinction to non-environmentalists, or as people who deploy a range of coping strategies in dealing with environmental problems. If environmentalists are to help in the course of managing these aspects of identity in wider society, then they must first come to recognise these aspects of identity in themselves. Highlighting the iatrogenic effects of some environmental campaigns will, we hope, therefore also serve the secondary function of reminding environmentalists that they too are sometimes inadvertently complicit in creating today's environmental problems.

The second element of the common strategies that we will discuss for each aspect of identity concerns *enabling factors*. As we noted at outset, human identity is formed in important part through interactions with one's society and culture. Thus, part of the reason that individuals take on identities that are environmentally problematic is that such identities are supported, and sometimes even encouraged, by the broader social context which, in turn, is importantly shaped by public policies. As Tim Jackson writes:

> Government policies send important signals to consumers about institutional goals and national priorities. They indicate in sometimes subtle but very powerful ways the kinds of behaviours that are rewarded in society, the kinds of attitudes that are valued, the goals and aspirations that are regarded as appropriate, what success means and the worldview under which consumers are expected to act. Policy signals have a major influence on social norms, ethical codes and cultural expectations. (Jackson, 2004: 117)

Environmental organisations may therefore attempt to address and 'disable' those features of society that currently promote the environmentally problematic aspects of identity.

Finally, each of the next three chapters will also present ways to *activate positive features of identity*. While thus far we have focused on those aspects of identity that contribute to environmental degradation, there are many aspects of the human psyche that can promote sustainability. For each of the three aspects of identity described in Part I, we will suggest ways that environmental organisations might work to encourage aspects of identity that serve as an 'antidote' to environmentally problematic features of identity, or that promote positive environmental behaviours and attitudes in and of themselves.

In sum, three common threads emerge in the treatment of each aspect of identity: tackle the iatrogenic effects of environmental campaigns; change those features of society that currently support the environmentally problematic aspects of identity; and promote those alternative aspects of identity that are environmentally beneficial.

Chapter 4

Shifting values and life goals

4.1 The basic strategy

As reviewed in Chapter 1, the empirical literature demonstrates that individuals who value money, possessions, achievement, power, image and status are less likely to engage in pro-environmental behaviours. They are also more likely to express negative attitudes towards the environment and to pursue environmentally damaging lifestyles. To address the environmentally problematic aspects of self-enhancing, materialistic values, Kasser (in press, b) suggests a two-fold strategy.

The first aspect of the strategy is to diminish those factors known to cause people to prioritise self-enhancing, materialistic values. Kasser and colleagues (2004) specified two main causes of the relatively strong adoption of materialistic, self-interested values. One is *social modelling*. Research shows that exposing people to messages promoting materialistic values tends to lead them to adopt such values themselves. For instance, studies have found that people express materialistic values more strongly when their peers or parents express these values, when they watch more television or are exposed to other forms of media, and when they live in a more economically competitive social and political context. *Psychological insecurity* is the second factor known to cause an orientation towards materialistic values. As we saw in Section 3.4, reminders of death increase people's orientation towards such values. Other forms of psychological insecurity that have been empirically associated with the adoption of such values include having emotionally cold, controlling parents, experiencing divorce as a child, feeling economically deprived, and even experiencing temporary hunger.

In addition to removing the causes of self-enhancing, materialistic values, Kasser (in press, b) proposes a second strategy: encourage values that are psychologically opposed to self-enhancing, materialistic values. Recall from Chapter 1 that substantial research suggests that values and goals exist in motivational systems that are organised in relatively consistent ways across cultures. Specifically, these studies have shown that some values and goals are typically experienced as being psychologically *consistent* with each other, and are thus relatively easy to simultaneously value and pursue, whereas other values and goals are in psychological *conflict* with each other. The extent of psychological consistency or conflict between values and goals can be represented statistically with *circumplex* models that align the values and goals people prioritise along the circumference of a circle, placing goals that are psychologically consistent near to each other, and goals that are in conflict on opposite sides of the circle. Figure 1 shows one such circumplex (based upon a study examining how 1,800 students from 15 nations rated the importance of a variety of life goals). As can be seen, the goals of financial success, image, and popularity cluster together, implying that if one of these extrinsic or materialistic goals is prioritised, people also tend to prioritise the other extrinsic, materialistic goals. *Intrinsic goals*, which concern pursuing self-acceptance (trying to grow as a person), affiliation (having good interpersonal relationships) and community feeling (trying to make the broader world a better place), are found on the opposite side of the circle. These goals tend to be antagonistic to the extrinsic goals: it is psychologically difficult for individuals to pursue both intrinsic and extrinsic goals simultaneously. Similar results are also achieved with another model. Using data from across 70 nations, Shalom Schwartz (2006) has found that self-enhancing values of power and achievement lie next to each other (i.e., are psychologically consistent) but are on opposite sides of the circumplex from values for self-direction (feeling free and choosing one's own goals), and the *self-transcendent* values of benevolence (being honest, helpful and loyal) and universalism (caring about the environment, a peaceful world and social justice).

Thus, this data suggests that one approach to diminishing the power of self-enhancing and materialistic values is to encourage people to place greater priority on values such as self-acceptance/self-direction, affiliation/benevolence and community feeling/universalism. What's more, the research reveals that such values both oppose environmentally damaging self-enhancing and materialistic values and promote more positive environmental attitudes and sustainable lifestyles (Kasser, in press, b).

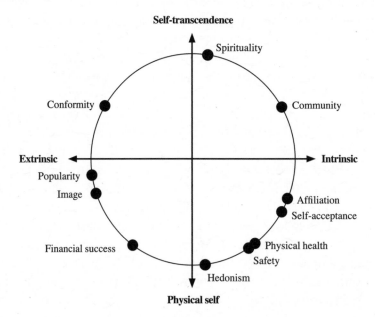

Figure 1

Circumplex model of values, based upon a study examining how 1,800 students
from 15 nations rated the importance of a variety of life goals (Re-printed from:
Grouzet et al., 2005 © American Psychological Association)

In sum, this two-pronged strategy suggests that as environmental organisations consider the best ways to reduce the detrimental environmental
effects of self-enhancing, materialistic values, they can work to: (i) decrease the
extent to which such values are modelled socially; (ii) help people cope with
feelings of insecurity in more adaptive ways; and (iii) develop programmes and
policies that promote intrinsic, self-transcendent values for personal growth,
close relationships and helping the broader world.

Clearly, this represents an agenda which extends far beyond the current
scope of most environmental organisations. In Chapter 8, however, we will
highlight some of the opportunities that identity campaigning offers for new
collaborations across civil society organisations working on a wide range of
different issues.

In the remainder of this chapter we will examine ways to decrease the social modelling of self-enhancing, materialistic values and to activate and encourage intrinsic values that are more likely to motivate pro-environmental concern and behaviour; we defer until Chapter 6 discussion of strategies to help people cope with feelings of insecurity in more adaptive ways.

4.2 Decreasing the social modelling of self-enhancing, materialistic values

4.2.1 Messages from environmental organisations

Unfortunately, rather than working to decrease the prevalence of self-enhancing, materialistic values, some environmental campaigns seem to reinforce such values.

Environmental organisations are urged, for example, to appeal to selfish desires as motivations for their audiences to engage in pro-environmental behaviour. Consider the following set of principles for environmental campaigners, developed through extensive consultation with environmental organisations:

> An accurate basic assumption might be that most people are essentially selfish, which is a natural human reaction and indeed a natural evolutionary process for any animal. Quality of life for oneself and one's dependants (sic) is always a key driving force for anyone. Any benefits from environmental behaviour, and there should be benefits from every environmental behaviour, must be tangible, immediate and specific to the person carrying out the behaviour. (Hounsham, 2006: 139)

In appealing to such selfish desires, particular emphasis is often placed upon the economic benefits of pursuing environmental goals. Consequently, the modern environmental movement is dominated by concepts that serve to reinforce the perception that non-human nature is an economic resource to be exploited. Take, for example: *the business case for sustainable development, payment for environmental services, the three pillars of sustainable development* or *green consumption*. To the extent that each of these concepts – all mainstays of much environmental campaigning – are emphasised, the environmental movement serves to reinforce the self-enhancing, materialistic values that, as shown in Chapter 1, are associated with more environmentally destructive behaviours.

Consider *the business case for sustainable development*, which risks reinforcing the perception that the pursuit of environmental goals should be abandoned when this departs from the pursuit of compelling business interests. Or consider *payment for environmental services*, an increasingly important trend in conservation, which is based on the assumption that where economic value can be assigned to ecosystems, then the imperative for conservation can be married with market ideologies. This approach reinforces materialistic goals: initiatives to place a monetary value on an ecosystem or a species reinforce the perception that financial interests are properly privileged above environmental ones. Such an approach is also likely to create problems when the economic case for environmental protection is difficult to make, when technological advances render the environmental service redundant, or when more money can be made exploiting a natural resource than conserving it. As Douglas McCauley writes:

> Conservationists] may believe that the best way to meaningfully engage policy-makers…
> is to translate the intrinsic worth of nature into the language of economics. But this is patently
> untrue – akin to saying that civil rights advocates would have been more effective if they
> provided economic justifications for racial integration. (McCauley, 2006: 28).

Or consider *the three pillars of sustainable development*, which equates social, environmental and economic outcomes, as though economic goals should be pursued in their own right and 'balanced' with social or environmental imperatives. Or finally, consider how *green consumption* and campaigns to 'buy green' reinforce the perception that the continued acquisition of new products is ultimately reconcilable with the need to address environmental problems, at a time when it is clear that a dramatic reduction in consumption is necessary on the part of most wealthier people.

We take heart that some in the environmental movement continue to speak out about the problems inherent in the promotion and elevation of materialistic, self-interested values above other values. For example, Gus Speth writes:

> The fundamental decision of today's environmentalism to work within the system… can
> be seen in hindsight as a major blunder. [In insisting] that the system can be made to work
> for the environment… scant attention is paid to the corporate dominance of economic and
> political life, to transcending our growth fetish, to promoting major lifestyle changes and
> challenging the materialistic values that dominate our society. (Speth, 2008: 5)

Bill Adams and Sally Jeanrenaud write:

> Much sustainability thinking has become path-dependent, locked into regulatory proce-
> dures and trapped by its own hopeful language of 'win-win'. The environmental move-
> ment's very acceptance at corporate and government tables has made it harder to express
> sustainability's uncomfortable challenges, harder to speak truth to power. (Adams and
> Jeanrenaud, 2008: 32)

And Jonathon Porritt calls for:

> a different level of engagement... and a much greater readiness to confront denial at every
> point, to challenge the slow, soul-destroying descent into displacement consumerism, and
> to take on today's all too dominant "I consume, therefore I am" mindsets and lifestyles.
> (Porritt, 2005: 309)

We agree with these analyses, but go further. We believe that it is crucial to add that the willingness with which mainstream environmentalism has
embraced self-enhancing, materialistic values and life goals *has actually served
to reinforce the dominance of these values and goals*, even when, as we saw in
Chapter 1, these are the very values and goals associated with more negative
environmental attitudes and more damaging environmental behaviour. As Clive
Hamilton writes:

> Much of the effort of environmentalists at shifting consciousness has focused on what is best
> described as 'green consumerism', an approach that threatens to entrench the very attitudes
> and behaviours that are antithetical to sustainability. (Hamilton, 2007: 10)

It thus seems likely to us that the environmental movement's rein-
forcement of these values and goals has contributed to the difficulties that the
movement currently experiences in forging systemic responses to compound
environmental challenges. We therefore believe that environmental organisations need to examine the values and goals reflected and promoted by their
communications and campaigns, so as to diminish the extent to which they
reinforce materialistic and self-enhancing values and goals.

While appeals to self-enhancing, materialistic values may undermine
the long-term aims of the environmental movement, other research makes it
clear that appeals to self-transcendent, intrinsic values present a more effective means of motivating pro-environmental behaviour. Although this is a very
important body of research, drawing on extensive empirical work in *self-determination theory*, we do not review it fully here. Typical of such studies is one

conducted by Maarten Vansteenkiste and colleagues (2004). In this experiment, students were asked to read a text about recycling. Subjects were randomly assigned to have this reading task framed as relevant either to the materialistic goal of saving money or to the intrinsic goal of benefiting the community. Results showed that those who had the goal framed in intrinsic terms not only learned the material in the text more deeply, but were also more likely to voluntarily visit the library and a recycling plant to learn more about recycling. For further discussion on the importance of self-determination theory for environmental communications and campaigns, see WWF (2008).

4.2.2 Policy approaches for reducing the social modelling of materialistic, self-enhancing values

In the last section, we focused on the empirical literature on values and goals, and the ways that this can inform how environmental organisations frame their communications and campaigns. There are, however, also ways in which environmental organisations, working in concert with other groups (see Chapter 8), can engage at a broader social level to decrease the extent to which society at large reinforces and encourages such values and goals. Governments play a crucial role in influencing peoples' values and goals, so to the extent that environmental organisations engage with governments, they should do so in awareness of the impact that the policy changes they seek will have on the broader social context. As Tim Jackson (2009) writes:

> [P]olicy shapes and co-creates the social world. So the idea that it is not only legitimate but possible for the state to intervene in changing the social logic of consumerism is far less problematic than is often portrayed. A critical task is to identify (and correct) those aspects of this complex social structure which provide perverse incentives in favour of a materialistic individualism. (p. 95).

A wide range of options are available in this regard but here we will briefly focus on two (see Jackson, 2009 for additional examples).

First, it is clear that advertisements and marketing are prominent means by which self-enhancing, materialistic values are encouraged. Underlying essentially every advertising message is the implicit proposition that purchase of a product or service can confer happiness or self-esteem. Government policy on advertising often operates to extend the reach and dissemination of these implicit messages. Laws in the US, for example, make advertising expenses tax-deductible for businesses.

Environmental organisations can begin to address these dynamics by developing and distributing educational materials that help individuals (and children in particular) to 'deconstruct' advertisements, recognising the techniques of persuasion that they deploy, and the links between pervasive materialistic values and environmental problems.

But environmental organisations should also support calls for legal restrictions on advertising. This could include campaigning for restrictions on advertising in public spaces (starting with advertisements in natural settings, perhaps), and campaigning for a ban on advertising to children, who – given that their cognitive skills and identities have yet to fully develop – are particularly susceptible to the persuasive techniques that advertisers use. There are precedents for both these approaches, as restrictions were recently placed on outdoor advertising in Sao Paulo, and there are laws restricting advertising to children in Sweden. Finally, environmental organisations could also campaign for the imposition of taxes on advertisements and increased support for public sector broadcasting.

A second type of strategy that environmental organisations could pursue is to support the development and implementation of new measures of national progress. Currently, most governments use gross domestic product, stock market indices and consumer confidence to assess national performance. Such measures are essentially based on financial transactions, business profit or consumer spending. It seems highly likely that the use of such measures tends to reinforce materialistic goals – particularly given the prominence that they are accorded in political discourse.

A number of alternative indicators have been proposed that would serve to introduce a wider range of values into public debate about national performance. These alternatives include proposals to directly measure citizens' psychological well-being, the Kingdom of Bhutan's gross national happiness measure, Redefining Progress' Genuine Progress Indicator (Talberth, *et al.* 2006) and the New Economics Foundation's Happy Planet Index (NEF, 2006). Although there are important differences between them, these alternative indicators all include variables that are not solely materialistic, but that instead reflect alternative values. For example, some of these indices include measures of social cohesion and trust, of life satisfaction and feelings of vitality, of volunteering and caring for others, and of environmental health. Were such alternative indicators to be widely adopted and reported, policy makers and citizens would receive a fundamentally different set of messages about national priorities. National debates would then be more likely to begin exploring the importance of well-being, social cohesion and sustainability.

4.3 Encouraging intrinsic and self-transcendent values

As we saw in Section 4.2.1, environmental organisations often retreat from ascribing value to nature beyond its utility in the pursuit of self-enhancing, materialistic goals. Instead, some of the clearest statements ascribing self-transcendent value to nature have come from politicians (who must deal daily with social concerns that cannot be reduced to economic parameters). The UK environment minister, Hilary Benn, for example, has said publicly that in his view "nature is part of our soul. I use the word soul because this is a fundamental part of all of us. Of our identity. Of where we come from." (Defra, 2008). Similarly, the UK Conservative MP Oliver Letwin has drawn attention to the need to instate beauty as a political value:

> A child who has no access to the grand scenes of the countryside, of the mountains and the lakes, of the cliffs and the sea, is deprived – not in the way in which a child whose parents are living hand to mouth in poverty is deprived, but in a different and important way...
> [T]he search for beauty is one of the great motivations of the human spirit. (Green Alliance, 2007: 44-45)

These are perceptions that should be explored publicly – and there is a crucial role for environmental organisations to help in such exploration. Unfortunately, mainstream environmentalism currently does little to support the development of these intrinsic and self-transcendent values, although we do recognise that some recent analyses of the failures of environmentalism have highlighted the need to infuse environmental debate with a different set of values (see, for example, Leiserowitz & Fernandez, 2008; Adams & Jeanrenaud, 2008; WWF, 2008), and WWF itself has supported practical projects aimed at exploring and strengthening these values amongst key stakeholders – through, for example, the Natural Change Project (WWF, in press). If environmental organisations can begin to discuss such values in a more open way and begin to develop policies that enhance them, intrinsic and self-transcendent values will become more legitimised in public discourse. As we have shown above, this, in turn, can be expected to promote more positive environmental attitudes and behaviours.

In considering approaches to promoting intrinsic and self-transcendent values, it is important to recognise that the relationship between the values individuals hold, and the behaviour they exhibit is a complex one. We have presented evidence that individuals who hold more intrinsic and self-transcendent values are more likely to engage in pro-environmental behaviour. Nevertheless, it is important to ask if further steps can be taken to strengthen the causal link between holding these values and making behavioural choices consistent with them. We suggest two approaches that may help in this regard: social support and the use of implementation intentions.

Social support. It is well recognised that social support is an important buffer against psychological stress, and support groups exist for numerous psychological problems, including having a terminally ill family member or being addicted to drugs. Such support groups have also been used to help people live more in concert with intrinsic and self-transcendent values. For example, Cecile Andrews (1998) has long worked with *simplicity circles* – groups of individuals who meet regularly to discuss the joys and challenges of trying to live a more materially simple life. Simplicity circles provide a place to share information and to learn new skills that can help people enact their intrinsic, self-transcendent values. But they also go a step further by providing people with support for a new set of norms about how to live their lives. That is, in a culture where consumerist messages dominate, members of simplicity circles receive support in attempting to base their decisions on a different set of values. Environmental organisations would do well to support groups of this kind, especially given that research demonstrates that those who have chosen to 'downshift' or pursue a 'voluntarily simple' lifestyle also live in more ecologically sustainable ways than do mainstream Americans (Brown and Kasser, 2005). WWF-UK delivered a project (funded by Defra) which explored the impact of providing a social learning space for groups of people to decide upon and implement their own changes towards more sustainable lifestyles. Connections between individuals were made explicit through discussions about their personal motivations for getting involved and what they felt most passionate about (Warburton, 2008). The critical importance of creating a community of interest was also highlighted by all participants in WWF-UK's Natural Change Project (WWF, in press) (see Section 5.4).

Implementation intentions. Another well-researched approach to help-ing people enact their goals comes from Peter Gollwitzer's (1999) impressive research program on *implementation intentions*. Studies inspired by this con-cept have demonstrated that people are more likely to behave in ways consistent with their stated goals when they have previously developed a very concrete *if-then* statement that helps them more easily identify situations where the goal is relevant, and that encourages them to engage in an appropriate behavioural response. Take, for example, an alcoholic who is attempting to stop drinking but who experiences social pressure to drink when he encounters some old drinking friends. Without a plan, the alcoholic can find himself susceptible to this pressure, but he is less likely to go drinking if he has previously developed an implementation intention such as: "If I am tempted to go to a bar, then I will immediately go instead to a café to get a coffee." Implementation intentions seem to help people *automatise* their behaviour so that they do not have to exert extra cognitive effort in thinking about what to do when a crucial choice arises. Some researchers have begun to apply this method to environmentally relevant behaviours. For example, implementation intentions have been effective in in-creasing compliance with speed limits (Elliott & Armitage, 2006), in decreasing the amount people drive (Eriksson *et al.*, 2008) and in increasing people's use of both public transportation and stores that sell sustainable products (Bamberg, 2002).

Environmental organisations could utilise research on implementation intentions in at least two ways. Firstly, they could begin to develop specific kinds of implementation intentions that connect very specific behaviours with posi-tive environmental values and goals, and then distribute these widely. Secondly, they could develop materials that introduce the concept of implementation in-tentions, with a view to equipping individuals to form their own environmen-tally helpful behavioural plans.

Chapter 5

Reducing prejudice towards non-human nature

5.1 The basic strategy

Chapter 2 reviewed evidence that connection to nature leads to greater motivation to engage in pro-environmental behaviour, but that the emergence of an environmental identity may be frustrated by in-group/out-group distinctions that people often make between humans and non-human nature.

An extensive body of empirical literature documents that people tend to be positively biased towards in-group members and often treat out-group members in prejudicial, discriminatory and sometimes aggressive ways. Some literature also suggests that these dynamics extend beyond commonly recognised forms of prejudice (racism, ethnocentrism, sexism), to include prejudice against other animals or nature.

While relatively little theory and research has specifically addressed the problem of developing practical responses to prejudice towards non-human nature, much is known about effective means of reducing prejudice and discrimination based on race, gender and sexual orientation. Because the literature tends to suggest that such interventions work for a variety of different types of out-groups, we have grounds for optimism that, where they can be applied, such interventions will also help to address prejudice towards non-human nature. Nonetheless, the application of these techniques to human-nature relationships is likely to entail specific challenges, and more work will be needed to refine these approaches.

The suggestions below are based on three different strands of research concerning the reduction of prejudice and stereotypes. The first strand concerns how people come to feel prejudice towards members of out-groups; here we will describe some ways in which environmental organisations may be inadvertently reinforcing prejudice towards non-human nature. The second strand concerns approaches to activating social values (such as empathy and egalitarian values) that are known to work in opposition to prejudicial beliefs and discriminatory behaviours between groups of humans. We will examine how such work might be relevant in the case of the human-nature relationship. Finally, we will discuss the *contact hypothesis*, a well-established approach built on the recognition that if members of in-groups and out-groups can be brought into contact under certain conditions, prejudice and discrimination can be lessened. We will reflect on the possible application of this approach to human-nature relationships.

5.2 Reducing prejudicial messages in society

5.2.1 The role of environmental organisations in increasing prejudice towards non-human nature

In their communications and campaigns, some environmental organisations may inadvertently exacerbate in-group/out-group distinctions between humans and nature, thereby undermining campaigns designed to motivate pro-environmental behaviour (or acceptance of pro-environmental policies) in the longer term. A prominent example of this is the difficulty some in the environmental movement – and some in the conservation movement in particular – experience in ascribing inherent value to individual animals or plants.[6] We touched on this problem in Chapter 4, in the context of the tendency to discuss nature and other species in instrumentalist terms, thereby reinforcing materialistic values.

The tendency of the environmental movement to take an anthropocentric perspective on nature is especially clear in the tension between the environmental and animal-welfare movements. It may be that environmental organisations fear that their popular and political support could be eroded through association with animal welfare campaigns, which are sometimes derided as 'sentimentalist' – precisely because they challenge in-group/out-group distinctions between humans and other animals. The fear that an environmental argument might be misconstrued as an animal-welfare argument even seems to lead environmental organisations to be unwilling to draw attention to environmental concerns that coincide with animal welfare concerns. For example, the intensive production of beef and pork can be opposed on both animal rights and environmental grounds, but our experience is that many environmental organisations feel discomfort highlighting the problems of factory farming or advocating vegetarianism, even when focussing exclusively upon the environmental (as opposed to animal welfare) issues arising from these industries. Indeed, this issue elicited strong responses from some reviewers of earlier drafts of this book, particularly environmentalists. This is unfortunate: as we saw in Chapter 2, addressing sources of prejudice towards other animals may be a prerequisite to engaging sources of prejudice towards non-human nature in general.

Environmental organisations – perhaps particularly those that are initiated and led from the North – often focus on the preservation of species, habitats or ecosystems, rather than on the individual animals or plants of which these are composed. Diversity is thus privileged above abundance (in other words, it is better to save a few rare animals than many ubiquitous ones), and the suffering of individual animals is often dismissed as a relatively unimportant issue. This tendency is quite explicit in environmental organisations' frequent indifference to the 'sustainable harvesting' of wild animals. Consider, for example, WWF's position on the Canadian seal cull:

> As long as the commercial hunt for harp seals off the coast of Canada is of no threat to the population of over 5 million harp seals, there is no biological reason for WWF-Canada to reconsider its current priorities and actively oppose the annual harvest of harp seals (WWF, 2004).

There are many other examples of tensions arising between conservation organisations and animal welfare groups on culling or hunting wild animals, and these often prompt intense public debate. At one level, the perspective taken by WWF in the case of the seal cull can be understood: it is not prudent for a conservation organisation to risk eroding its public support in a country (particularly such as Canada) where there is widespread acceptance of the seal cull. And yet, in retreating from a position that could otherwise help to legitimise public empathy towards seals, this stance may serve to further exacerbate in-group/out-group distinctions, which as we saw in Chapter 2, seem to create barriers to delivering environmental goals.

It may well serve the purposes of environmental organisations to begin to dismantle the barriers that separate the animal welfare and environmental movements. In particular, it seems likely that when environmental organisations dismiss opposition to culling wild animals, this will weaken public opposition to, for example, clear felling old-growth forests. To an environmental scientist there may be an important distinction here (based on a concern for the preservation of species diversity – whereas the seals may 'grow back', the forest will not, and a whole ecosystem will be lost with it). But to a member of the public, motivated to engage with both animal welfare and environmental issues on empathic grounds, this distinction may be lost.

Whereas depreciating the value of individual animals may tend to exacerbate the perceived distinction between humans and non-human animals, there are also more direct ways in which conservation organisations may work unwittingly to increase this prejudice. The activities of conservation organisations may inadvertently serve to frustrate the emergence of environmental identity (see Chapter 2), through the 'objectification' of biodiversity.

The perception that humans are separate from nature is likely to be heightened both by conservation activities that frame the natural world as something that does not include humans or from which humans must be excluded, and by interventions that serve to reinforce an instrumentalist view of nature (that is, a view which holds that nature exists solely as a source of raw materials for human activities). As Sian Sullivan (2006) writes: "'Biodiversity' is constructed as an object both when nature is set aside in national parks and when community-based and other conservation initiatives focus on increasing the money to be made from viewing and consuming the objects of nature" (p.126).[7]

Rather than emphasising the need for nature either to be 'left alone', or to be exploited commercially, environmental and conservation organisations might place greater emphasis on the type of *relationship* that conservation programmes establish between local people and non-human nature. Sullivan suggests that this is a very *realistic* approach to take, since it derives "from witnessing peoples' despair and depression... over the inability of pragmatic development and governance bodies to converse with these... concerns and desires" (p.128). An alternative approach to conservation, she suggests, will reflect an acknowledgement that biological diversity is linked to cultural diversity in knowledge, languages and practice, and that sustaining both these forms of diversity is necessary for ecological and cultural wellbeing. It is certainly WWF-UK's experience, in working with partners worldwide, that the need for *relationship and conversation* is often more strongly expressed amongst communities in the field than in policy debate in national capitals. If conservation practice in less industrialized countries is to come to reflect this, however, it will probably be best achieved through the work of small and local organisations rather than large conservation organisations based in more industrialized countries.

5.2.2 Confronting misconceptions within society that frustrate the emergence of environmental identity

While it appears that humans have a natural tendency to categorise individuals on the basis of their sex or race, the evidence also shows that the attitudes people form towards those in different categories are to a large extent learned.

That is, although young children do often differentiate between sex and race, only later do they come to think that one group (usually their own) is 'better'. In part this occurs through direct teaching by parents and other adults, but more often it arises through social modelling and exposure to messages in the media (Whitley & Kite, 2006).

Among the messages children sometimes learn that support prejudice and discrimination are *legitimising myths* which serve to justify displaying prejudices against particular groups of people: groups may be portrayed as less intelligent, or lazier, or inherently more aggressive and violent. Researchers have found that such stories are a key component of a widely examined predictor of prejudice and discrimination called *social dominance orientation* (SDO), "the extent to which one desires that one's in-group dominates and is superior to out-groups" (Pratto *et al.*, 1994: 742). A large number of studies have documented that individuals high in SDO express more negative attitudes towards a wide range of out-groups, including members of other races, sexes, sexual orientations, castes and political groups (Whitley & Kite, 2006). At least one study has shown that college students displaying higher levels of SDO are significantly more likely to endorse and personally use "products made by injuring or killing animals" (Hyers, 2006: 200).

Lauri Hyers has examined the stories that people use to legitimise such behaviours, producing results of importance to environmental campaigning. The most frequent justification that participants in her study gave for using animals was "necessity". Many individuals reported that a healthy diet requires injuring and killing animals, or that using animals in these ways was justified on practical and economic grounds. It seems probable that a similar set of justifications would be reported in the course of explaining exploitation of non-human nature more widely.

It is important, therefore, that where they are based on factual misrepresentations, these legitimising stories are rebutted, particularly in the education of children. Environmental organisations could campaign for provisions within school curricula to debate these legitimising stories, such as the perceived necessity of animal-based protein in a healthy diet. Other ways to confront legitimising stories can be adapted from the methods used to raise awareness about racist and sexist depictions in the media. For example, environmental organisations could highlight instances when commercial messages, news reporting and governmental pronouncements reflect messages supportive of the objectification or commodification of nature.

While each of these efforts seems to us to hold some promise, some of the legitimising stories that support humans' prejudice towards non-human nature are likely to require more intensive interventions of the sort described in Sections 5.3 and 5.4 below.

5.3 Activating positive social values

While thus far we have focussed on how societal messages can frustrate the emergence of environmental identity, the literature also makes it clear that intra-personal factors and personality differences are another source of prejudicial values and behaviours. Among the large array of personality differences that have been explored over the years, two closely related variables have been consistently associated with lower levels of prejudicial attitudes towards a variety of out-group members. The first is empathy, "an other-oriented emotional response congruent with another's perceived welfare; if the other is oppressed or in need, empathic feelings include sympathy, compassion, tenderness, and the like" (Batson *et al.*, 1997: 105). The second is egalitarian values, or the priority one places on treating other people equally and giving them equal opportunities; this value has even been called "the prejudice antidote" (Biernat *et al.*, 1996: 155) because of its power in reducing prejudice

Both variables are important from an environmental perspective. Steps can be taken towards increasing empathy for other animals and non-human nature. People high in empathy tend to be low in materialistic values and high in intrinsic values (Sheldon & Kasser, 1995). They also tend to display lower levels of prejudice across a number of different types of out-groups, including African Americans, Native Americans, Arabs, Australian Aborigines, lesbians, gay men, obese individuals, and feminists (Whitley & Kite, 2006). Such findings suggest that similar results could be achieved when these personality factors are examined as predictors of prejudice towards non-human nature.

While it would of course be both philosophically and practically problematic to seek equality between humans and other animals, the importance of egalitarian values in tackling prejudice between humans underscores the importance of acknowledging that non-human nature should be valued in its own right: that is, it has value which extends beyond its usefulness to humans.[8] The recognition of the inherent value of nature is likely to generate dividends analogous to those achieved through increasing the prevalence of egalitarian values in engaging prejudice towards human out-groups.

Experimental evidence suggests that prejudice and discrimination against human out-groups decline when egalitarian values and empathy are *activated* in people's minds. For example, a long tradition of research has examined how to activate egalitarian values with a method called *value confrontation*, developed by Milton Rokeach (1973). In this method individuals receive feedback making them aware of discrepancies between their egalitarian values and either their behaviour or the egalitarian values of their peers. Such feedback seems to create an uncomfortable emotional state to which individuals respond by attempting to bring their values and behaviour into alignment. While there is some controversy about the optimal conditions for this procedure, recent research suggests it can be quite effective for individuals who endorse egalitarian values but nonetheless still hold some prejudicial attitudes towards out-groups (Son Hing & Zanna, 2002). In applying these approaches to build awareness of the inherent value of nature, environmental organisations should perhaps initially target those groups who already have close contact with the non-human natural world in a non-exploitative way, but who do not consistently express an environmental identity in their behavioural choices. For example, it may be that gardeners, ramblers or pet owners will be especially likely to respond well to value-confrontation interventions.

Another potentially powerful intervention has been developed by Daniel Batson and colleagues (e.g. Batson *et al.*, 2002). These researchers have conducted a series of studies in which subjects listen to an interview with a person, and are then asked either to take an "objective" and "detached" perspective towards how the person feels without considering his/her emotional state, or to "try to feel the full impact" of what someone has been through and imagine how that person "feels about what has happened and how it has affected his life". Researchers have found that this relatively simple intervention increases empathy for groups as diverse as drug dealers, older people, African Americans, AIDS patients and the homeless, with consequent declines in prejudice towards these individuals (Whitley & Kite, 2006).

At least one study has explored the effects of perspective-taking on environmental concern (Schultz, 2000). Experimental subjects were shown pictures of wild animals being harmed (a seal caught in a fishing net, for example). Some study participants were asked, in observing these pictures, "to imagine how the subject in the images feel" and "to take the perspective of the subjects" whereas other participants in the control group were asked to "take a neutral perspective, being as objective as possible about the subjects". After viewing the pictures, subjects were asked to complete a questionnaire developed to assess the basis of their wider environmental concerns: that is, whether these concerns arose solely because of a concern about their own personal welfare, because of effects on other people, or because of their concern for all living things. Subjects who were asked to take the animals' perspective were found to express significantly higher levels of biospheric environmental concern (concern for all living things) than participants instructed to remain objective. Much as with research exploring human out-groups, it seems that the process of perspective-taking may have generated feelings of empathy and therefore a greater concern for the welfare of non-human nature.

5.4 Improving contact between species

It has long been recognised as simplistic to assume that prejudice between humans groups can be reduced simply by bringing them together (Allport, 1954; Pettigrew, 1998). However, it does seem clear that, under some conditions, contact can reduce the anxiety associated with meeting others different from oneself, create empathy for out-group members, and lead people to re-categorise in-groups and out-groups into a 'we' identity, that is, to form a super-ordinate group (Whitley & Kite, 2006).

Creativity and flexibility will be needed to adapt techniques developed in the context of human interactions to human-nature interactions. Understanding the experiential factors that promote a sense of environmental identity will be critically important here, yet little research has been conducted on these. At one level, there are opportunities for indirect contact, and well-produced films, books and video games could help promote a stronger sense of connection to nature. But these are unlikely to substitute for real-life contact with animals and nature.

In the longer term, childhood experience will be important. But a child's relationship with nature is unlikely to be promoted through approaches to 'environmental education' that insist on the quantification or objectification of nature. Childhood experience of nature should become a core element of children's education – such that adolescents leave formal education equipped with a conceptual framework that enables them to relate to their own experiences of nature, a vocabulary with which they feel comfortable in discussing their relationship with nature, and educational experiences that lead them to identify nature as something in which they are immersed even in an urban environment (for example, through the air they breathe, the water they drink, and the people they encounter). The benefits of such education may well extend beyond the environmental dividends. Evidence suggests that helping individuals, particularly children, to develop an experiential sense of their connection to the natural world helps to foster the emergence of socially and psychologically balanced individuals. Indeed, many studies identify direct experience of the outdoors as having therapeutic value (Mind, 2007; Morris, 2003; Seymour, 2003).

The strongest impacts are likely to be created through approaches to wilderness experience that build on the techniques of ecopsychology, though programmes that attempt to provide this have yet to become fully integrated into the strategies deployed by mainstream environmental organisations. WWF has used such techniques in the Natural Change Project (WWF, in press), a process of personal transformation and reflection through nature-based workshops that ran for participants in Scotland drawn from the business, education, arts, and charitable sectors. The project deployed a wide range of psychological approaches and mindfulness exercises, but at its heart lay a dawn till dusk solo experience in nature. Such solitary encounters with nature have a very long and culturally diverse history (often popularised and oversimplified through Native American associations).[9]

The Natural Change Project adapted and incorporated techniques from Joanna Macy's *'the work that reconnects'* (e.g. Macy and Brown, 1998). This is a programme of group exercises that are designed to provide opportunities to share personal responses to the condition of the world, and to promote empathy with other living things. Amongst these powerful techniques, an exercise that Macy calls the 'Council of All Beings' perhaps particularly responds to the need to create greater empathy between human and non-human life, as it provides an opportunity for participants "to step aside from... [their] human identity and speak on behalf of other animals" (p.161). These techniques have been used to great effect in a number of other initiatives; the rapidly growing Transition Movement (Hopkins, 2008), for example, draws upon variations of Macy's techniques in its training courses.

Chapter 6
Promoting healthier coping with fear and threats

6.1 The basic strategy

In Chapter 3 we discussed a third environmentally problematic aspect of identity: people's responses to unpleasant emotions such as fear, anxiety, guilt and existential angst, and to threats to their self-esteem and identity coherence. When reminded of environmental threats and of their own death, people often respond in ways that are environmentally problematic, diverting their awareness from the threats, reinterpreting the threats in self-serving ways, becoming apathetic about the problems, or activating materialistic values and in-group/ out-group aspects of identity also known to undermine positive environmental values and behaviours.

In order for environmental organisations to develop means of intervening with regard to this third environmentally problematic aspect of identity, it may be helpful to understand how some psychotherapists approach the treatment of individuals who experience unpleasant emotions or threats to their identity and who attempt to cope in maladaptive ways (such as through alcohol intake or passive-aggressive behaviours).

Here, we will highlight three fundamental steps that a psychotherapist might take to helping an individual who is experiencing unpleasant emotions and who is not coping optimally.[10]

The first step is to help the individual become aware of the existence of the coping strategy or defence mechanism. Clients are often unaware of their use of these strategies, and are frequently resistant to therapists' proposals that these strategies are problematic because, from the clients' point of view, these strategies reduce stress or the immediate angst that they experience. As we saw in Chapter 3, Homburg and colleagues' (2007) results demonstrate that the coping strategies of seeking pleasure, denying guilt, and relativisation were each associated with significantly *lower* levels of reported stress from environmental problems. Nevertheless, even when such coping mechanisms do reduce stress, it is incumbent upon the therapist to help increase awareness of them when they also yield maladaptive ways of behaving. For example, a stiff drink can certainly help calm a person after a stressful day, but when used too frequently, this means of coping can become maladaptive.

In the second step, having helped the client to acknowledge the use of coping strategies, the therapist and client now begin to process the unpleasant thoughts, feelings and threats against which the coping strategy offered protection. At this stage, as the coping strategies are dismantled, the client may feel upset, depressed or angry. While these emotions are no doubt unpleasant to experience, most therapists recognise that it is crucial for clients to have the opportunity to express such emotions, as the expression of unpleasant emotions is typically a good indicator of the eventual success of a therapy process. The therapist's most important role here is to provide an empathic, non-judgmental environment for the client to explore and express the feelings against which he or she was previously defending.

In the third stage, the therapist helps the client find new and better ways of managing and coping with threats and unpleasant emotions. Psychotherapy cannot forever remove all the past pain a client has experienced, nor can it protect against all future pain. But therapy can help people to cope with past and future threats in ways that reduce the threat and unpleasant feelings, and in ways that promote recovery rather than magnify and maintain the threats.

In addition to these three steps, many psychotherapists and sociologists acknowledge that it is important to address the ways that both the direct interpersonal environment and the broader social environment may promote certain types of defence mechanisms or coping strategies. For example, Cooper (1998: 958) notes that defence mechanisms are "constantly influenced and shaped by the immediate interpersonal context". Such dynamics may arise from the ways that families teach the use of coping strategies (e.g. overeating, denial or blaming others). They may also arise when therapists' own discomfort with certain emotions or defensive proclivities lead them to promote (or fail to confront) their clients' defence mechanisms. This is commonly referred to as *counter-transference*. Sociologists such as Hochschild (1979) go even further, emphasising that broader social structures and social models render some means of emotional management acceptable and others unacceptable; for example, cultures vary in the extent to which they encourage public demonstration of grief following bereavement. Thus, from this perspective, a fourth approach to intervening with defence and coping mechanisms is to once again be alert to their presence in broader social messages, including environmental campaigns.

6.2 Reducing environmentally problematic defence and coping mechanisms

6.2.1 The three psychotherapeutic steps

What insights can the therapeutic process outlined in Section 6.1 offer environmental organisations in the course of helping people cope with the threats and fears posed by environmental challenges?

First, environmental organisations can be alert to instances where people and organisations engage in defence mechanisms that risk reducing levels of engagement in positive environmental behaviour. Environmental organisations can then *gently and empathically* point out the existence of these strategies. An understanding of effective behaviour change strategies suggests that it will be ineffectual to bemoan public apathy, or admonish individuals for deploying particular coping mechanisms. Because such approaches are themselves threatening, they are likely to increase resistance to positive behaviour change (Miller & Rolnick, 2002). Public attacks on coping mechanisms may also erode trust in environmental organisations, further undermining their effectiveness.

A better approach would acknowledge the emotions underlying the maladaptive coping strategy. For example, diversion strategies can be acknowledged through statements of empathy, conveying the sense that "we understand that global warming is scary and people don't want to think about it...". Similarly, apathy can be acknowledged through statements that convey the recognition that "we know some of these problems seem so overwhelming that people (including us, sometimes) just want to give up...".

By intervening in these ways, environmental organisations can state truths that often remain unspoken – global warming *is* scary and people often *do* feel hopeless. Moreover, such interventions convey a sense of understanding and even acceptance, and thereby help people begin to recognise that they may be attempting to manage their emotions in ways that are ultimately not adaptive for themselves or the environment. By demonstrating a sense of empathy and understanding, environmental organisations will be better placed to build public trust and rapport.

Second, environmental organisations can help people to *express* the emotions that they feel about environmental destruction. Environmental organisations frequently present information (often very scary information) about environmental challenges with little emotional content or context. This is perhaps analogous to a therapist who dryly recites the symptoms and aetiology of a client's disorder without attending to his or her emotional response to this information. Alternatively, environmental organisations sometimes adopt a confrontational stance in an attempt to provoke strong public emotion. This is perhaps analogous to a therapist who quickly attacks a client's psychic structure without having first established his or her trust. Such therapists often find that their clients become resistant and defensive, or that they do not return for future therapy sessions.

Recall that the task at this second stage is to help clients express what they are feeling, no matter how unpleasant. The relevance of this stage for environmental organisations is reinforced by Homburg and colleagues' (2007) findings that those subjects who report unpleasant emotions such as anger and sadness in response to environmental stresses are more likely to engage in positive environmental behaviours. It seems that even the opportunity to deeply explore thoughts and feelings associated with death can help in this regard. As was reviewed in Section 3.4, brief reminders of death are known to lead people to orient towards the materialistic values that promote environmental degradation (at least within a cultural context where materialistic values dominate). However, other studies have shown that a more sustained, reflective meditation on the feelings aroused by thoughts of death can actually *decrease* materialistic strivings (Cozzolino *et al.*, 2004; Lykins *et al.*, 2007). Usually, when people are reminded of their own death, they quickly suppress the associated thoughts and emotions (Arndt *et al.*, 2004; Kosloff & Greenberg, 2009). But when reflection on death is sustained, this process can perhaps be forestalled, bringing about greater sense of meaning in life, and a shift towards the self-transcendent and intrinsic values discussed in Chapter 4.

These empirical findings, as well as decades of clinical practice, suggest that in order to help activate positive environmental behaviours, environmental organisations will ultimately need to develop approaches that help people express the fear, anger, sadness, angst or sense of threat from environmental challenges that many are probably already experiencing (whether consciously or otherwise). Again, we emphasise that this is *not* to advocate the provocation of such unpleasant feelings through confrontational communications or campaigns. Rather, we suggest that environmental organisations should attempt to develop a trusting and empathic rapport with key stakeholders, providing opportunities for people to begin to explore and express the unpleasant feelings they have about environmental challenges. Such efforts could occur through the kinds of support groups described in Section 4.3 above, or approaches drawing on understandings of ecopsychology (see Section 5.4). The work of Joanna Macy, mentioned above, offers a particularly well-developed approach to helping people work through their despair about environmental destruction, and these techniques have been taken up and adapted by other practitioners.[11] Another approach that mixes art and psychotherapy is the Altars to Extinction project, which provides a physical place for individuals to reflect on, and grieve for, species that have gone extinct (Gomes, 2009).

With regard to the third step in the therapeutic process, environmental organisations can help people develop positive coping strategies that are less likely to lead to a worsening of an individual's environmental impact. For example, Sections 3.4 and 3.5 showed that people often activate culturally sanctioned and highly valued aspects of their identity in response to threats. This fact further reinforces the importance of the interventions described in Chapters 4 and 5: If social norms supporting materialism are reduced and intrinsic goals become more dominant, and if people become less likely to express prejudice towards non-human nature, then it is more likely that environmentally beneficial norms will be activated under conditions of environmental threat. Some empirical evidence supports this perspective. In Section 3.5 we reviewed work demonstrating that participants in forest management games tended to exploit simulated natural resources less sustainably when they had been reminded of their mortality. Mark Dechesne and colleagues (2003) found that this effect disappeared when people were provided with an alternative means of coping with the fear of their own death: in this case, thinking about the possibility of an afterlife. Again, these findings suggest that environmental organisations would do well to work to promote intrinsic, pro-social values in society and new ways of understanding and empathising with non-human life, especially to the extent that they can help people turn towards these values under times of threat.

Environmental organisations might also want to work to develop the types of coping strategies that the literature suggests usually have *adaptive* effects (Zeidner & Endler, 1996). Two types of strategy will be discussed here: *problem-focused coping* and *emotion-focused coping*.

The first type, *problem-focused coping*, entails strategies in which the individual actively attempts to change the situation that is giving rise to the source of stress. Homburg and colleagues (2007) found that one of the best predictors of engaging in positive environmental behaviours was endorsing this *problem-solving* coping strategy. This strategy entailed seeking out more information and educating oneself about the environment, as well as talking with other people and seeking out social support (see the discussion of support groups in Chapter 4). Environmental organisations sometimes encourage this type of strategy, through the provision of concrete information about actions that can be undertaken to reduce an environmental threat – although the provision of social support networks is less common. It should be noted, however, that Homburg and colleagues found problem-solving strategies to be associated with increased levels of reported stress from an awareness of environmental challenges. Thus, problem-solving, while perhaps helpful in motivating beneficial environmental behaviours, may not reduce unpleasant emotions.

The second type of coping strategy that the empirical literature highlights as typically beneficial is called *emotion-focused coping*. In this form of coping, individuals do not attempt to engage the source of stress, but instead attempt to change their emotional reactions to it. Of course, this could serve to encourage the more environmentally problematic ways of coping described in Chapter 3. But one emotion-focused strategy that might be particularly useful for environmental organisations is the cultivation of *mindfulness*, or an acceptance of one's experience as it is in the moment. The cultivation of mindfulness has a long history in Buddhism as a means of reducing suffering in life, and contemporary scientists have recently developed secular mindfulness training techniques to help people cope with pain, anxiety and depression (Gerner *et al.*, 2005). Not only is mindfulness effective in reducing psychological distress, but some evidence suggests that it can also benefit the environment. For example, across four studies, Brown and colleagues (2009) found that mindfulness was associated with reduced desire for materialistic attainments, and Brown and Kasser (2005) found that more mindful people were less likely to endorse materialistic values and more likely to endorse intrinsic values. Moreover, even after statistically controlling for the effects of subjects' values, Brown and Kasser found that adults who were more mindful engaged in more positive environmental behaviours and had lower ecological footprints than individuals less attuned to, and accepting of, the present moment. Thus, another useful strategy that environmental organisations could undertake is to adapt existing techniques for cultivating mindfulness as an approach to helping people cope with environmental threats.

6.2.2 Eliminating environmental messages that promote ecologically destructive coping mechanisms.

As we have noted, environmental organisations will need to be alert to instances where communications and campaigns (either their own, or those of other organisations) encourage the adoption of defence and coping mechanisms that tend to exacerbate environmental problems. As a first step in this, environmental organisations should examine their own communications.

For example, Renée Lertzman (2007) recently deconstructed a social marketing campaign that urged individuals to petition for government action to safeguard water quality in the Great Lakes. The campaign is in many ways typical of many 'in-your-face' environmental communications: it features a photograph of a girl looking across a lake, alongside a sign reading: "Warning: No More Swimming. No More Fishing. No More Drinking Water. NO MORE GREAT LAKES." About this advertisement, Lertzman writes:

> The Lakes are presented as vulnerable, finite, and gravely threatened. There is the sense that unless we do something now, we risk losing such magnificent resources forever… We are presented with a choice to act, but if we consider how such images may touch people on an affective, potentially unconscious level, can we safely assume this is necessarily an impetus to act? … We need as communicators to be more aware of the psychic dimensions of these issues if we want to comprehend what it means to learn about and respond to serious ecological issues. This includes work in psychoanalysis and psychology on issues of guilt, loss, mourning, and anxiety that can inform how people respond to messaging and campaigns. (Lertzman, 2007: 4-5; emphasis in original)

Highlighting the scale and finality (or *irreparability*) of an environmental threat may therefore be counterproductive. This possible effect is likely to be further exacerbated by communications that increase mortality awareness (see Section 3.4). For example, communications on climate change that stress the danger of extinction, civil strife, or widespread death and disease must be designed carefully for this reason. This is *not* to argue that communicators should 'dumb down' the scale of impact of environmental problems. It is important to fully disseminate an understanding of such impacts, but this should probably not be done in a way that is deliberately designed to stimulate fear. Further, to the extent that fears and threats are activated, it will be to the advantage of environmental organisations to encourage coping with these in the more adaptive ways we have described above.

In addition to the apathy and fear that result from some environmental campaigns, it is likely that other types of environmental communications and campaigns sometimes serve to increase the likelihood that unhelpful psychological coping responses, such as those outlined in Chapter 3, are triggered. Consider, for example, the frequent insistence that environmental challenges such as climate change can be met through the cumulative effects of individuals adopting 'simple and painless lifestyle changes' (checking their tyre pressures, or switching their TV off standby, for example). The direct additive impact of large numbers of individuals changing their behaviour in ways that lead to small reductions in their personal environmental impacts will be a small reduction in overall environmental impact (McKay, 2008). However, it also seems likely that communications which exaggerate the environmental impact of simple and painless steps might actually serve to encourage individuals to deploy such strategies for diversion (see Section 3.1), thereby leaving them less inclined to adopt other, more difficult and perhaps environmentally significant, behavioural changes (see also WWF, 2009).

Another potentially counterproductive approach is to blame other social groups or nationalities (whether explicitly or implicitly). The foregoing analysis suggests that such campaigns might: (i) increase the sense of threat of those individuals who are targeted, and therefore increase the likelihood that the targeted individuals will deploy environmentally problematic coping strategies; and (ii) lead those who do not belong to the groups that are singled out to engage in projection (i.e. deny their own responsibility and feelings of guilt, and instead identify other groups to blame) (see Section 3.2).

Consider, for example, a UK direct action campaign against urban 4x4s (also called SUVs). This campaign has the aim "to make driving a big 4x4 in town as socially unacceptable as drink-driving". The campaign provides reasons not to drive an urban SUV:

> Our descendants will be left to deal with the effects of climate change caused by our profligate use of fossil fuels. Drivers of 4x4s should start editing their photo albums now … The aggressive look of a big 4x4 means other people on the road may make assumptions about the person behind the wheel. In an ordinary car, you won't get dirty looks from all and sundry when you drive around town.[12]

The campaign encourages direct action against owners of SUVs, such as issuing SUVs with spoof parking tickets that "contain lots of information for urban 4x4 drivers about the effects of their choice of vehicle on the rest of us".[13]

This campaign has certainly been highly successful in terms of the press coverage and public debate that it has generated, and may have contributed to building the support of non-SUV drivers for punitive government measures against SUV drivers (increases in road tax, for example). But this campaign may also have had some unfortunate secondary effects. First, we are sceptical that the campaign would have encouraged many drivers of SUVs to part with their vehicles, as those SUV drivers who felt threatened by the campaign are likely to have deployed other coping strategies (many of which may have caused further damage to the environment). Second, and more importantly, this campaign may actually have discouraged non-SUV drivers (of whom there are far more) from taking steps to minimise their own contribution to traffic-related pollution by driving less or parting with their car completely. That is, vilifying SUV drivers may promote denial of the guilt that drivers of smaller cars could otherwise feel, by encouraging projection of this guilt onto SUV drivers. As such, the campaign could have served to *increase* overall traffic-related emissions.

Summary of Part II

We have proposed that the environmental movement, in its efforts to change the policies and practices of governments and businesses, and the behaviours of individuals, neglects an important third level of intervention: human identity. We have reviewed theoretical arguments and empirical data documenting that three aspects of human identity (i.e. self-enhancing and materialistic values and goals, in-group/out-group dynamics, and responses to fear and threat) often contribute to environmentally problematic values and behaviours. We have also presented a variety of strategies to: (i) reduce the iatrogenic effects of some environmental campaigns; (ii) disable the ways that society currently encourages these environmentally problematic aspects of identity; and (iii) activate those aspects of identity that promote positive environmental attitudes and behaviours. These strategies are summarised in Table 1.

In Part III of this book, we suggest some other benefits that adoption of identity campaigning might provide.

Table 1
Summary of identity-based campaign strategies for environmental challenges

• Avoid language and campaigns that reinforce materialistic, self-enhancing values.

• Frame environmental messages to connect with intrinsic values, rather than extrinsic or materialistic values.

• Address the societal influence of advertising, for example by supporting: (i) media literacy programmes; (ii) the removal of advertising from public spaces (especially natural settings); (iii) bans on marketing to children; and (iv) policies to tax advertising at higher rates.

• Promote the development and use of alternative indicators of national progress that include values other than materialism.

• Create community groups to support the adoption of materially simple and ecologically sustainable lifestyles. Creating a safe environment where participants are given permission to openly express their deepest fears about environmental issues will be important here.

• Help people create implementation intentions to increase the likelihood of behaving in ways that are consistent with intrinsic, self-transcendent values.

• Avoid messages suggesting that the lives of individual animals are of little significance.

• Build an awareness that humans are themselves part of nature, and confront society's stories that legitimise prejudice towards non-human nature.

• Develop programmes to activate an awareness of the inherent value of nature and empathy for non-human nature (perhaps initially addressing gardeners, ramblers or pet owners).

• Develop means of increasing optimal contact between humans and non-human nature, including indirect contact, environmental education programmes that promote an experiential sense of connection to nature, and by drawing on the techniques of ecopsychology.

• Gently point out when society and individual people use coping strategies to avoid confronting environmental concerns, and acknowledge the emotions that underlie these strategies.

• Help people *express* their fear, sadness, angst and anger about environmental destruction, rather than *provoking* such feelings. Group work will be important here.

• Help people activate intrinsic and self-transcendent values when they feel threatened by environmental challenges.

• Promote problem-focused coping strategies and the emotion-focused coping strategy of mindfulness to help people cope with environmental threats.

• Design environmental campaigns to minimise the risk that people will be led to deploy environmentally problematic coping strategies.

PART III:
REASONS TO BE CHEERFUL:
NEW OPPORTUNITIES OFFERED
BY IDENTITY CAMPAIGNING

Chapter 7

Four good things about identity campaigning

7.1 Aspects of identity can be engaged and changed

We have attributed global environmental challenges to fundamental aspects of human identity, and we are convinced that, given the necessary public engagement and political leadership, these aspects of identity can be effectively managed.

Arguments that humans are in some way evolutionarily predisposed to be materialistic, to denigrate nature, or to respond to fear in destructive ways are sometimes used to suggest that the best strategies that environmental organisations can deploy are to attempt to exploit those areas of convergence between short-term self-interest and environmental imperative. In fact, there are compelling arguments against pressing evolutionary biology into service to support approaches to environmental campaigning that takes human selfishness as its starting point.

Firstly, while biologists have long argued about whether aspects of the human psyche are more influenced by nature or nurture, the current consensus is that most aspects of human identity (and the human psyche more broadly) are shaped by both genetic and cultural factors. This said, in the case of the three aspects of identity discussed in this book, the evidence actually suggests that cultural influences play a particularly important formative role: the extent to which people endorse materialistic values seems to have little to do with genetics and much more to do with social experiences (Giddens, *et al.*, 2009; Kasser *et al.*, 2004); whilst people do seem predisposed to categorise others, the evaluations they attach to those categorisations are largely learned (Whitley & Kite, 2006); and the means by which people cope with threat is largely shaped by messages received from their culture (Hochschild, 1979; Greenberg *et al.*, 2004).

But we are *not* trying to deny any heritable components to the phenomena we have explored in this book. Rather, we are arguing that even though there may well be a genetic component to these three environmentally problematic aspects of identity, it seems that cultural factors also have a critically important role in shaping them.

This leads us to a second reason for being optimistic that these aspects of our identities can be effectively engaged: recognising that these environmentally problematic aspects of human identity may have an important genetic basis does not imply that they cannot be managed. Ascribing an evolutionary basis to a characteristic or aspect of identity does not necessarily imply biological determinism. As Richard Dawkins suggests:

> From a Darwinian point of view, the problem with sustainability is this: sustainability is all about long-term benefits of the world or of the ecosystem at the expense of short-term benefits. Darwinism encourages precisely the opposite values. Short-term genetic benefit is all that matters in a Darwinian world... [But] this is not a reason for despair, nor does it mean that we should cynically abandon the long-term future... and get our noses down in the trough of short-term greed. What it does mean is that we must work all the harder for the long-term future, in spite of getting no help from nature, precisely because nature is not on our side...
>
> It is a manifest fact that the brain – especially the human brain – is well able to over-ride its ultimate programming; well able to dispense with the ultimate value of gene survival and substitute other values. (Dawkins, 2001; 8-11)

Although Dawkins' view does not hold out a great deal of hope, there are some persuasive arguments that human morality may not necessarily represent a 'thin veneer' overlaid, through human culture, on fundamentally selfish natures. Indeed, there is evidence that humans and our closest relatives in the natural world may share traits commonly ascribed to a moral sensibility (see, for example, de Waal, 2006). But, even accepting Dawkins' more gloomy perspective, it is clear that the only ethical approach to addressing the collective problems created by some aspects of our identities (even those that have an important genetic or evolutionary component) is to intervene culturally. Indeed, this is how people throughout the centuries have always attempted to address the more problematic aspects of the human psyche. Fortunately, as we have seen, there is good evidence that all of these aspects of the human psyche can be managed to an important extent.

7.2 Engaging identity and values is an effective way of creating sustained behavioural change

There is growing recognition within the environmental movement of the importance of values in driving behavioural change, and we hope that this book will add to that understanding. Of course, it is not necessarily the case that, in changing a person's attitude towards something, this will also change his or her behaviour. This disparity between *attitudes* and *behaviours* has been well publicised, and has been called the attitude-behaviour gap. So, for example, Rose and Dade (2007) write that:

> Behaviour is generally a strong determinant of opinion… This is why one cannot drive be-haviour with information based on opinion" (p.1) and people "adopt 'views' which explain or are consonant with our behaviours, even if the topic appears to be one of 'simple fact'. The reasons we do this… all boil down to being driven by values (p.7).

Differences of opinion emerge, of course, on whether the best strategy is to work with existing values (trying to make a particular environmental campaign 'fit' with these values) or to work to influence these values themselves. Here our views diverge markedly from those who suggest that environmental campaigns should be framed to appeal to self-interested or materialistic values (see WWF 2008 for a full discussion of this debate). Designing campaigns to appeal to existing self-interested or materialistic values may lead to short-term and piecemeal behaviour change, but, as we have seen in this book, such an approach runs the risk of undermining more fundamental attempts to address systemic environmental challenges. We therefore believe that this is a strategy that environmental organisations would do best to avoid. On the other hand, as we have also seen, there is extensive experimental evidence showing that pro-environmental behaviour is related to certain values and aspects of identity, and that these can be meaningfully managed through a range of interventions. Many of these interventions will draw, of course, on techniques with which today's environmental campaigners are already very familiar.

7.3 Non-governmental organisations can have influence disproportionate to their resources

Many of the interventions that we propose in this book can be undertaken without the need for additional resources, and this is particularly true of our suggestions for minimising iatrogenic effects. But more importantly, it should be recognised that non-governmental organisations are able to influence public and political debate in a way that is disproportionate to the resources at their disposal – because of the trust that they command.[14] Unsurprisingly, many studies show that the receptivity of an audience to a message depends largely upon the perceived credibility and trustworthiness of the messenger (Druckman, 2001). Businesses that invest extensively in the use of public relations companies are well aware of the importance of the perceived interests of the messenger – and deploy the *third party technique* by using public relations agencies to separate the message from what could be construed as a messenger with vested interests.

Many of the strategies we have presented, particularly those in Chapter 6, will have the benefit of increasing public trust of environmental organisations. Moreover, it seems likely that appeals to the more environmentally beneficial aspects of people's identity, such as empathy and egalitarian values, will improve the public's sense of rapport with environmental organisations, and hence their receptivity to environmental campaigns.

This influence can be further extended by achieving clarity and consistency in the values that underpin the work of non-governmental organisations. Drawing on cognitive science and neuroscience, several academics have recently highlighted the importance of achieving clarity on the values underlying a campaign – see, for example, Lakoff (2004) and Westen (2007). This is something to which we turn in the next chapter.

7.4 Even seemingly unsuccessful campaigns can help change aspects of identity

In working towards specific goals (creating new policy, or motivating a change in behaviour) environmental communicators and campaigners typically activate particular *frames* in the brains of their audience. Frames are the mental structures (physically enshrined in neural networks) that enable people to make sense of reality and that determine what individuals each see as 'common sense'. Frames "structure our ideas and concepts, they shape the way we reason, and they even impact how we perceive and how we act" (Lakoff, 2006: 20). Moreover, they are largely unconscious. Social institutions and situations are shaped by mental structures (or frames), but frames are also propagated by social institutions.

According to the cognitive scientist George Lakoff, messages can be characterised by both *surface framing* and *deep framing*. Surface framing refers to catchy slogans and clever spin. Deep framing refers to forging the connections between a debate or public policy and a set of deeper values or principles. Surface framing (crafting particular messages focussing on particular issues) cannot work unless these messages resonate with a set of long-term deep frames.

There is a mutual process by which our social institutions and situations shape our frames, which in turn shape our institutions. Public policy, for example, has an important implication for the frames that predominate in society. Recognition of this led Lakoff and co-workers at the Rockridge Institute to distinguish two types of policy – *material policy* and *cognitive policy*:

> Material policy consists of the nuts and bolts, what is done in the world to fulfil policy goals. Cognitive policy is about the values and ideas that both motivate the policy goals and that have to be uppermost in the minds of the public and the media in order for the policy to seem so much a matter of common sense that it will be readily accepted (Brewer and Lakoff, 2008a: 1).

Policy proposals that may seem similar at the more 'superficial' level of material policy can differ widely in terms of cognitive policy. These differences may be implicit, drawing on (and supporting) a set of deep frames without conscious discussion. Differences in cognitive policy may arise, for example, in the extent to which policies rely upon market mechanisms to address environmental problems. Putting a financial value on an endangered species, and building an economic case for its conservation, risks its commodification. It makes the species equivalent to other assets of the same value (a hotel chain, perhaps). This is a very different cognitive policy than one that attempts to achieve the same conservation goals through the ascription of inherent value to such species – as something that should be protected in its own right. As Brewer and Lakoff suggest:

> Concentrating on material criteria alone can be counterproductive if a policy is either unpopular, or if it instils in the public's mind long-term values that contradict the aims of the policy (Brewer and Lakoff, 2008b: 3).

Environmental organisations should therefore be aware of the cognitive implications of their campaigns in at least two ways.

Firstly, they should recognise that campaigns for new policies or regulations, if successful, will lead to new government interventions which will themselves have important cognitive implications. Irrespective of whether or not these policies are helpful in immediately alleviating a set of environmental problems, they are likely to either support or undermine work on the longer-term task of engaging the aspects of identity that we have outlined.

Secondly, even if a campaign is unsuccessful, it will have cognitive impacts – because people will see the campaign materials and unconsciously respond to the deep frames that these enshrine. These cognitive impacts may be unrelated to the specific environmental issue or policy request that the campaign is highlighting. Thus, the way in which the campaign is framed is likely to have unforeseen secondary impacts on deep frames – and these may either help or hinder the emergence of more systemic environmental concern.

These points have profound implications for environmental campaigning. Working with an understanding of cognitive policy can help to ensure that the public *experience* of new environmental policies simultaneously serves to convey and reinforce the deep frames necessary for systemic engagement with environmental challenges. Such an understanding can also be used to design campaign communications that have a widespread positive impact in shaping the deep frames that promote environmental sustainability, even if the policy campaign itself is unsuccessful. Through an understanding of the cognitive impacts of environmental campaigns, environmental organisations can identify interventions that contribute to long-term success – even when they may fail in immediate policy terms.

Such an approach will require changes in current monitoring and evaluation processes. So long as the success of environmental campaigns is defined solely in terms of short-term material policy outcomes, it may be difficult to encourage cognitive policy goals to be built into them.

Chapter 8

Beyond the environment: opportunities for new coalitions

In addition to helping reinforce identities and values that will provide a long-term benefit to the environmental movement, the approach we have proposed here provides multiple opportunities for building new coalitions. To us, this is one of the most important aspects of this publication, and a particularly exciting implication of the approach that we are advocating.

We recognise that the proposals we have made for engaging dominant values and aspects of identity are ambitious, and the environmental movement will not be able to make progress in this way whilst working alone. But there is a very high level of coincidence between the values and aspects of identity that currently frustrate systemic responses to environmental challenges and the values and identities that frustrate delivery on a range of other challenges such as war, aggression, poverty, racism, homophobia, sexism, prejudice against the disabled, the abuse of human rights, and indifference to animal welfare. Although it is beyond the scope of this little book to build this case in detail, the empirical literature clearly suggests that the same aspects of identity are of crucial importance to addressing a wide range of challenges. For example, the research clearly shows that self-enhancing, materialistic values are not only associated with more negative environmental attitudes and behaviours, but also with less concern for social justice, equality, and a world at peace, less pro-social behaviour, and more manipulative, competitive behaviour (see Kasser *et al*., 2007). Similarly, the tendencies that promote prejudice towards non-human nature probably span numerous other out-groups (Whitley & Kite, 2006). As Marjorie Spiegel (1996) writes: "Any oppression helps to support other forms of domination. That is why it is vital to link oppressions in our minds, to look for the common, shared aspects, and work against them as one" (p.30). What's more, maladaptive responses to fear and threats not only create a tendency towards problematic environmental behaviour, but also towards a number of other problematic social behaviours, such as aggression or victimisation of out-groups (Greenberg *et al*., 2004; Stephan & Stephan, 2000). Thus, these findings show that issues of concern to diverse third sector organisations often stem from the same underlying aspects of human identity.

Of course, third sector organisations often do collaborate across different agenda. For example, environment and development organisations sometimes collaborate on a range of issues (and there are forums which have been established specifically to explore common policy agenda). But typically these collaborations centre on a convergence of interest on particular policy demands, for example, climate change or international trade policy. In contrast, we are not aware of campaigns that forge alliances across third sector organisations in order to focus on engaging the aspects of identity we have been describing here. We see two ways such coalitions might operate: by forming prominent coalitions to campaign for policy change with important identity impacts, and by striving for consistency in the values that must come to underpin the changes for which a range of third sector organisations campaign. We now examine each of these approaches in a bit more detail.

8.1 Prominent coalitions on policy with identity impacts

Third sector organisations can form prominent coalitions on policy in order to address aspects of identity that lead to a broad array of problematic outcomes. Organisationally, this approach would be similar to current collaborations on campaigns for specific policy interventions (for example, reducing greenhouse-gas emissions or regulating the arms trade). However, the campaigns we foresee would be explicitly focussed on elements of material policy (see Section 7.4) to engage societal practices that support and enable problematic aspects of identity. For example, a broad coalition of third sector organisations might decide to collaborate on strengthening regulations governing advertising to children. Research has shown that young children are cognitively and psychologically susceptible to advertising – they typically do not understand the notion of intent to sell, and frequently accept advertising claims at face value (Linn, 2004). Studies also have found that exposure to commercial television increases children's scores on assessments of materialistic values (Nairn *et al.*, 2007; Schor, 2004), which, as we have seen, leaves them more antagonistic to a range of pro-environmental and pro-social concerns. Further, exposure to marketing messages is also known to contribute to a host of other problems for young people, including alcohol and cigarette use, eating disorders, violence and sexual promiscuity (Linn, 2004; Schor, 2004). Given the range of unfortunate outcomes associated with marketing to children, there is scope for a broad coalition of third sector

organisations (e.g. organisations concerned with child welfare, human development, human rights, animal welfare and the environment) to campaign for
a ban on advertising to young children. As we noted earlier, such restrictions
on advertising are already in place in some Scandinavian countries, and were
actually considered in the US in the 1970s before being defeated by a coalition
of marketers and companies with vested interests.

8.2 Establishing consistency in the values underpinning third sector campaigns

A second approach to building new coalitions could focus on the cognitive impacts of campaigns (see Section 7.4), without attempting to pursue specific common policy outcomes. Accordingly, a range of different organisations might
agree on a set of deep frames that they want to promote, and then use their different policy campaigns as vehicles to convey these. According to some political
scientists, this is the approach that the American political Right took with great
success from the Ronald Reagan to George W. Bush administrations:

> Conservative think tanks, over the past three decades, have been extremely successful in
> pure cognitive policy, that is, in shaping public discourse to lead the public to accept basic
> conservative values and principles. That long-term investment has paid off in making mate-
> rial conservative policies seem natural (Brewer and Lakoff 2008b: 1).

Such concerted *cognitive campaigning* could proceed without the development of any formal alliances between organisations on specific policy
issues, but would require agreement on the deep frames that they seek, jointly,
to embed. This publication, we hope, begins to make clear which deep frames
it would be best to avoid and which it would be best to support.

The third sector as a whole has thus far failed to develop a common
understanding of these deep frames and to recognise the benefits of coming to
collectively frame their respective campaigns in this way. This probably helps
explain the difficulty that the sector experiences in building public support and
pressure for new and ambitious policy programmes.

8.3 Conclusion

We of course believe that it is crucial for environmental organisations to continue campaigns for certain environmental policy changes and to attempt to motivate particular private-sphere behavioural change. At the same time, we hope that it is clear that an understanding of identity campaigning points to the need to carefully review current strategies if these are to contribute more effectively to creating the systemic changes that are needed and if they are to avoid counterproductive effects. Moreover, we see an understanding of identity campaigning leading to an appreciation of other new and important ways in which the environmental movement could engage, and which it currently neglects.

All told, we believe that the environmental movement cannot fully contribute to creating the systemic changes needed in response to today's environmental challenges unless it understands the problems posed by values and identity, and unless it promotes environmentally beneficial aspects of identity at a societal level.

ENDNOTES

1 'Regulatory chill' refers to the tendency for many new regulatory proposals never to be discussed in policy circles because of the recognition that these will not be politically feasible. The barriers placed in the way of the emergence of new environmental regulation by current political priorities cannot therefore be properly assessed in terms of proposals for new regulation that are seen publicly to have failed. Many regulatory proposals will never make it to the stage of public discussion.

2 This indifference about the reasons why people adopt a behavioural change is particularly prevalent in approaches to environmental campaigns that are based on commercial marketing techniques. For a full discussion of the importance of the *reasons* to which environmental campaigners appeal in the course of motivating pro-environmental behavioural change, and for a critique of some marketing approaches, see WWF (2008).

3 Debate persists in the psychological literature about the distinction between values and goals. Throughout this book, we have tried to be consistent in using the terminology adopted by the authors of the studies we cite.

4 Note that Schwartz uses 'achievement' to denote the desire to demonstrate one's success relative to that of others. This is potentially misleading, because people may also strive to achieve things in pursuit of intrinsic goals. But we adopt Schwartz's use of achievement throughout this book.

5 Advertisement running in British press for the new television channel 'Watch', October 2008.

6 It may be preferable to refer to the 'intrinsic value' of nature, rather than the 'inherent value' of nature here (see Curry, 2006). However, we choose to use 'inherent value' in order to avoid possible confusion with the intrinsic goals of self-acceptance, affiliation and community feeling, about which we write elsewhere in this book. In referring to the 'inherent value of nature', we denote the value that nature has as an *end in itself*, rather than as a means to an end, irrespective of whether or not such value is contingent upon a valuer.

7 There are signs that the debate between, on the one hand, proponents of the separation of humans and nature, and, on the other, advocates of alternative community-led approaches to conservation, is moving on. An emerging and parallel discussion now focuses on political ecology (the study of the interactions between the way nature is understood and the politics and impacts of environmental action) (Adams and Hutton, 2007). In this debate, which explores the compatibility of conservation and human welfare, nature or resource-focused approaches are contrasted with people-centred approaches. Although resource-focused approaches tend to view 'political' constraints as outside their control, they recognise the limitations these place on their plans. On the other hand, people-centred approaches (e.g. rights-based and sustainable livelihoods approaches) integrate political considerations into their analysis. People-centred approaches recognise that conservation is a social process with social impacts, and would ideally ensure that local *world views* (e.g. respecting the inherent value of nature) played an influential role in shaping any intervention. In practice, however, particularly where northern or international conservation or environmental NGOs are driving the agenda, this rarely happens.

8 We believe that it is not possible to extend the principle of egalitarianism to our relationship with non-human animals. But this must not preclude recognition that non-human animals and nature have inherent value. The equal right of all life forms to live and flourish (also called 'Biocentric egalitarianism') is, as Curry (2006) argues, "both intellectually and metaphysically implausible – why should value in nature be distributed equally or evenly? (Ironically, there is almost a mechanistic quality to the assumption that it is.) [Such egalitarianism] is also hopelessly impracticable as a guide to action: you cannot ask anyone (let alone everyone) to live as if literally every life-form – a lethal virus, say – has equal value to all others... and it offers no guidance, indeed allows no way, to resolve inevitable conflicts." (pp. 75-76). But, in recognising this, we need not conclude that human interests should always take precedence over those of other life forms: indeed, in according nature inherent value, we must accept that there will be some instances where the interest of non-human nature should be privileged above that of humans.

9 Participants wrote extensively about the impact of this experience in their blogs, which are available at www.naturalchange.org.uk

10 It should be re-emphasised that, in the course of learning from approaches that have been refined by psychotherapists, we are not suggesting that the emotional management strategies discussed in Chapter 3 are in any way abnormal. Quite the reverse – they are entirely ubiquitous, and, as we have seen, may be effective in managing stress. Nor are we suggesting that those who work for environmental organisations have successfully escaped these emotional management strategies. Indeed, it seems clear that environmental communicators and campaigners should challenge themselves, on an ongoing basis, to recognise the full scale of environmental problems, and to constantly review the proportionality of their responses. It is also important that those working for environmental organisations frequently reflect on the ways in which their organisations contribute to perpetuating environmental problems – both as an inevitable result of being functioning economic entities (that hold investments, heat their buildings and transport their staff) and as a result of the unintended but sometimes deleterious impacts of their campaigns.

11 In the UK, for example, see the work of David Key and Mary-Jane Rust.

12 See: http://www.stopurban4x4s.org.uk/reasons.htm (Accessed 20/02/09).

13 See: http://www.stopurban4x4s.org.uk/help.htm (Accessed 20/02/09).

14 The 2009 Edelman Trust Barometer found NGOs to be the most trusted institution in every region other than Asia Pacific: "Around the world, NGOs are the only institution trusted by more than 50% of informed publics" (Edelman, 2009: 8).

REFERENCES

Adams, W.M., & Hutton, J. (2007) People, parks and poverty: Political ecology and biodiversity conservation. *Conservation and Society, 5*, 147-183

Adams, W.M., & Jeanrenaud, S.J. (2008) *Transition to Sustainability: Towards a Humane and Diverse World.* IUCN, Gland, Switzerland.

Allport, G.W. (1954) *The Nature of Prejudice.* New York: Perseus.

Andrews, C. (1998) *The Circle of Simplicity.* New York: Harper Collins.

Arndt, J., Cook, A., & Routledge, C. (2004) The blueprint of terror management: Understanding the cognitive architecture of psychological defense against the awareness of death. In J. Greenberg, S.L. Koole, & T. Pyszczynski (Eds.) *Handbook of Experimental Existential Psychology* (pp. 35-53). New York: Guilford Press.

Arnocky, S., Stroink, M., & De Cicco, T. (2007) Self-construal predicts environmental concern, cooperation, and conservation. *Journal of Environmental Psychology, 27*(4), 255-264.

Bamberg, S. (2002) Effects of implementation intentions on the actual performance of new environmentally friendly behaviours – results of two field experiments. *Journal of Environmental Psychology, 22*, 399-411.

Batson, C.D., Polycarpu, M. P., Harmon-Jones, E., Imhoff, H.I., Mitchener, E. C., Bednar, L.L., Klein, T.R., & Highberger, L. (1997) Empathy and attitudes: Can feelings for a member of a stigmatized group improve feelings toward the group? *Journal of Personality and Social Psychology, 72*, 105-118.

Batson, C.D., Chang, J., Orr, R., & Rowland, J. (2002) Empathy, attitudes, and action: Can feeling for a member of a stigmatized group motivate one to help the group? *Personality and Social Psychology Bulletin, 28*, 1656-1666.

Baumeister, R.F., Dale, K., & Sommer, K.L. (1998) Freudian defense mechanisms and empirical findings in modern social psychology: Reaction formation, projection, displacement, undoing, isolation, sublimation, and denial. *Journal of Personality, 66*, 1081-1124.

Beatson, R.M., & Halloran, M.J. (2007) Humans rule! The effect of creatureliness reminders, mortality salience, and self-esteem on attitudes towards animals. *British Journal of Social Psychology, 46*, 619-632.

Biernat, M., Vescio, T.K., Theno, S.A., & Crandall, C.S. (1996) Values and prejudice: Understanding the impact of American values on outgroup attitudes. In C. Seligman, J.M. Olson, & M.P. Zanna (Eds.) *The Psychology of Values* (pp. 153-189). Mahwah, NJ: Erlbaum.

Bragg, E.A. (1996) Towards ecological self: Deep ecology meets constructionist self-theory. *Journal of Environmental Psychology, 16*, 93-108.

Brewer, J. & Lakoff, G. (2008a) Comparing climate proposals: A case study in cognitive policy. Unpublished paper. Available at: www.cognitivepolicyworks.com

Brewer, J. & Lakoff, G. (2008b) Why voters aren't motivated by a laundry list of positions on issues. Unpublished paper. Available at: www.cognitivepolicyworks.com

Brown, K.W., & Kasser, T. (2005) Are psychological and ecological well-being compatible? The role of values, mindfulness, and lifestyle. *Social Indicators Research, 74*, 349-368.

Brown, K.W., Kasser, T., Linley, P. A., Ryan, R.M., & Orzech, K. (2009) *When what one has is enough: Mindfulness, financial desire discrepancy, and subjective well-being.* Manuscript under review.

Clayton, S. (2003) Environmental identity: A conceptual and an operational definition. In S. Clayton & S. Opotow (Eds.) *Identity and the Natural Environment* (pp. 45-65). Cambridge, MA: MIT Press.

Cooper, S.H. (1998) Changing notions of defense within psychoanalytic theory. *Journal of Personality, 66*, 947-964.

Cozzolino, P., Staples, A.D., Meyers, L.S., & Samboceti, J. (2004) Greed, death, and values: From terror management to transcendence management theory. *Personality and Social Psychology Bulletin, 30*, 278-292.

Cramer, P. (1991) *The Development of Defense Mechanisms*. New York: Springer-Verlag.

Curry, P. (2006) *Ecological Ethics: An Introduction*. Cambridge, UK: Polity.

Dawkins, R. (2001) Sustainability doesn't come naturally: a Darwinian perspective on values. Inaugural Lecture of The Values Platform for Sustainability, The Environment Foundation, delivered on 14 November 2001.

Dechesne, M., Pyszczynski, T., Arndt, J., Ransom, S., Sheldon, K.M., van Knippenberg, A., & Janssen, J. (2003) Literal and symbolic immortality: The effects of evidence of literal immortality on self-esteem striving in response to mortality salience. *Journal of Personality and Social Psychology, 84*, 722-737.

de Waal, F.B.M. (2006) *Primates and Philosophers: How Morality Evolved*. Princeton, NJ: Princeton University Press.

Defra (2008) Speech by Rt Hon Hilary Benn MP at the Barnes Wetlands Centre: Why the natural environment matters – 21 July 2008.

Druckman, J.N. (2001) On the limits of framing effects: Who can frame? *The Journal of Politics, 63*(4), 1041-1066.

Dutcher, D.D., Finley, J.C., & Luloff, A.E. (2007) Connectivity with nature as a measure of environmental values. *Environment and Behaviour, 39*(4), 474-493.

Edelman (2009) *2009 Edelman Trust Barometer*. Available at: www.edelman.com/trust/2009

Elliott, M. A., & Armitage, C.J. (2006) Effects of implementation intentions on the self-reported frequency of drivers' compliance with speed limits. *Journal of Experimental Psychology: Applied, 12*, 108-117.

Emmons, R.A. (1989) The personal strivings approach to personality. In L.A. Pervin (Ed.) *Goal Concepts in Personality and Social Psychology* (pp. 87-126). Hillsdale, NJ: Erlbaum.

Eriksson, L., Garvill, J., & Nordlund, A.M. (2008) Interrupting habitual car use: The importance of car habit strength and moral motivation for personal car use reduction. *Transportation Research Part F: Traffic Psychology and Behaviour, 11*, 10-23.

Feather, N.T. (1992) Values, valences, expectations, and actions. *Journal of Social Issues, 48*, 109-124.

Frantz, C.M., Mayer, F.S., Norton, C., & Rock, M. (2005) There is no "I" in nature: the influence of self awareness on connectedness to nature. *Journal of Environmental Psychology, 25*(4), 427-436.

Freud, A. (1936) *The Ego and the Mechanisms of Defense*. New York: Hogarth Press.

Freud, S. (1923/1961) The ego and the id. In J. Strachey (Ed. & Trans.) *The Standard Edition of the Complete Works of Sigmund Freud* (Vol. 19, pp.12-66). London: Hogarth Press.

Gatersleben, B., Meadows, J., Abrahamse, W., & Jackson, T. (2008) Materialistic and environmental values of young people. Unpublished manuscript. University of Surrey, UK.

Gerner, C.K., Siegel, R.D., & Fulton, P.R. (Eds.) (2005) *Mindfulness and Psychotherapy*. New York: Guilford Press.

Giddens, J.L., Schermer, J.A., & Vernon, P.A. (2009) Material values are largely in the family: A twin study of genetic and environmental contributions to materialism. *Personality and Individual Differences, 46*, 428-431.

Goldenberg, J., Kosloff, S., & Greenberg, J. (2006) Existential underpinnings of approach and avoidance of the physical body. *Motivation and Emotion, 30*, 127-134.

Goldenberg, J., Pyszczynski, T., Greenberg, J., Solomon, S., Kluck, B., & Cornwell, R. (2001) I am not an animal: Mortality salience, disgust, and the denial of human creatureliness. *Journal of Experimental Psychology: General, 130*, 427-435.

Gollwitzer, P. (1999) Implementation intentions: Strong effects of simple plans. *American Psychologist, 54*, 493-503.

Gomes, M. (2009) Altars of extinction: Honoring the broken circle of life. In L. Buzzell & C. Chalquist (Eds.) *Ecotherapy: Healing with Nature in Mind*. (pp. 219-223). San Francisco, CA: Sierra Club Books.

Good, J. (2007) Shop 'til we drop? Television, materialism and attitudes about the natural environment. *Mass Communication and Society, 10*, 365-383.

Green Alliance (2007) *A Greener Shade of Blue? Reflections on New Conservative Approaches to the Environment.* London: Green Alliance.

Greenberg, J., Arndt, J., Simon, L., Pyszczynski, T., & Solomon, S. (2000) Proximal and distal defenses in response to reminders of one's mortality: Evidence of a temporal sequence. *Personality and Social Psychology Bulletin, 26*, 91-99.

Greenberg, J., Koole, S., & Pyszczynski, T. (Eds.) (2004) *Handbook of Experimental Existential Psychology.* New York: Guilford Press.

Grouzet, F.M.E., Kasser, T., Ahuvia, A., Fernandez-Dols, J.M., Kim, Y., Lau, S., Ryan, R.M., Saunders, S., Schmuck, P., & Sheldon, K.M. (2005) The structure of goal contents across 15 cultures. *Journal of Personality and Social Psychology, 89*, 800-816.

Hamilton, C. (2007) Self-creation under consumerism and the transition to an ecological consciousness. Unpublished manuscript.

Hewstone, M., Rubin, M., & Willis, H. (2002) Intergroup bias. *Annual Review of Psychology, 53*, 575-604.

Hirsh, J.B., & Dolderman, D. (2007) Personality predictors of consumerism and environmentalism: A preliminary study. *Personality and Individual Differences, 43*, 1583-1593.

Hochschild, A. (1979) Emotion work, feeling rules, and social structures. *American Journal of Sociology, 85*, 551-575.

Homburg, A., Stolberg, A., & Wagner, W. (2007) Coping with global environmental problems: Development and first validation of scales. *Environment and Behaviour, 39*, 754-778.

Hopkins, R. (2008) *The Transition Handbook: From Oil Dependency to Local Resilience.* Totnes, UK: Green Books.

Hounsham, S. (2006) *Painting the Town Green: How to Persuade People to be Environmentally Friendly.* London, UK: Green Engage.

Hyers, L.L. (2006) Myths used to legitimize the exploitation of animals: An application of Social Dominance Theory. *Anthrozoos, 19*, 194-210.

Jackson, T. (2004) *Motivating Sustainable Consumption: A Review of Evidence on Consumer Behaviour and Behavioural Change.* Report to the Sustainable Development Research Network, Centre for Environmental Strategy, University of Surrey.

Jackson, T. (2009) *Prosperity Without Growth? The Transition to a Sustainable Economy.* London: Sustainable Development Commission.

Kals, E., Schumacher, D., & Montada, L. (1999) Emotional affinity toward nature as a motivational basis to protect nature. *Environment and Behaviour, 31*, 178-202.

Kasser, T. (2002) Sketches for a self-determination theory of values. In E.L. Deci & R.M. Ryan (Eds) *Handbook of Self-determination Research* (pp.123-140). Rochester, NY: University of Rochester Press.

Kasser, T. (2005) Frugality, generosity, and materialism in children and adolescents. In K.A. Moore & L.H. Lippman (Eds.) *What do Children Need to Flourish?: Conceptualizing and Measuring Indicators of Positive Development* (pp.357-373). New York: Springer Science.

Kasser, T. (in press a) Cultural values and the wellbeing of future generations: a cross-national study. *Journal of Cross-cultural Psychology.*

Kasser, T. (in press b) Values and ecological sustainability: Recent research and policy possibilities. In J.G. Speth & S. R. Kellert (Eds.) *Toward a New Consciousness: Creating a Society in Harmony with Nature.* New Haven, CT: Yale School of Forestry and Environmental Studies.

Kasser, T., Cohn, S., Kanner, A.D., & Ryan, R.M. (2007) Some costs of American Corporate Capitalism: A psychological exploration of value and goal conflicts. *Psychological Inquiry, 18*, 1-22.

Kasser, T., Ryan, R.M., Couchman, C.E., & Sheldon, K.M. (2004) Materialistic values: Their causes and consequences. In T. Kasser & A.D. Kanner (Eds.) *Psychology and consumer culture: The struggle for a good life in a materialistic world* (pp.11-28). Washington DC: American Psychological Association.

Kasser, T., & Sheldon, K.M. (2000) Of wealth and death: Materialism, mortality salience, and consumption behaviour. *Psychological Science, 11*, 352-355.

Koole, S.L., & Van Den Berg, A.E. (2004) Lost in the wilderness: Terror management, action orientation, and nature evaluation. *Journal of Personality and Social Psychology, 88*, 1014-1028.

Kosloff, S., & Greenberg, J. (2009) Pearls in the desert: Death reminders provoke immediate derogation of extrinsic goals, but delayed inflation. *Journal of Experimental Social Psychology, 45*, 197-203.

Lakoff, G. (2004) *Don't think of an Elephant: Know Your Values and Frame the Debate.* Vermont: Chelsea Green.

Lakoff, G. (2006) *Thinking Points: Communicating our American Values and Vision.* Available at: www.rockridgeinstitute.org

Lazarus, R.S. (1991) *Emotion and Adaptation.* Oxford: Oxford University Press.

Leiserowitz, A.A., & Fernandez, L.O. (2008) *Towards a New Consciousness: Values to Sustain Human and Natural Communities. A Synthesis of Insights and Recommendations from the 2007 Yale F&ES Conference.* Yale School of Forestry and Environmental Sciences.

Lertzman, R. (2007) Exploring Anxious Dimensions of the Irreparable: Considerations from Psychoanalysis. Paper delivered at: "Twenty-Five Years After the Die is Cast: Mediating the Locus of the Irreparable", The 9th Biennial Conference on Communication and the Environment, DePaul University, Chicago IL, 22-25 June 2007.

Lertzman, R. (2008) The myth of apathy. *Ecologist, 19*(6), 16-17.

Leyens, J-P., Rodriguez-Perez, A., Rodriguez-Torres, R., Gaunt, R., Paladino, M-P., Vaes, J., & Demoulin, S. (2001) Psychological essentialism and the differential attribution of uniquely human emotions to ingroups and outgroups. *European Journal of Social Psychology, 31*, 395-411.

Light, A. (2000) What is an ecological identity? *Environmental Politics, 9*(4), 59-81.

Linn, S. (2004) *Consuming Kids: The Hostile Takeover of Childhood.* New York: The New Press.

Lykins, E.L.B., Segerstrom, S.C., Averill, A.J., Evans, D.R., & Kemeny, M.E. (2007) Goals shifts following reminders of mortality: Reconciling posttraumatic growth and terror management theory. *Personality and Social Psychology Bulletin, 33*, 1088-1099.

Macy, J., & Brown, M.Y. (1998) *Coming Back to Life: Practices to Reconnect Our Lives, Our World.* British Colombia: New Society Publishers.

Marshall, G. (2007) *Carbon Detox: Your Step-by-Step Guide to Getting Real About Climate Change.* London: Gaia.

Mandel, N., & Heine, S.J. (1999) Terror management and marketing: He who dies with the most toys wins. *Advances in Consumer Research, 26*, 527-532.

Mayer, F.S., & Frantz, C.M. (2004) The connectedness with nature scale: A measure of individuals' feeling in community with nature. *Journal of Environmental Psychology, 24*, 503-515.

McCauley, D.J. (2006) Selling out on nature. *Nature, 443*, 27-28.

McKay, D. (2008) *Sustainable Energy – Without the Hot Air.* Cambridge, UK: UIT.

Miller, W.R., & Rollnick, S. (2002) *Motivational Interviewing: Preparing People for Change* (2nd Ed.). New York: Guilford Press.

Mind (2007) Ecotherapy: *The Green Agenda for Mental Health.* Mind week report, London, May 2007.

Morris, N. (2003) *Health, Well-Being and Open Space: Literature Review.* OPENspace, Edinburgh, July 2003.

Nairn, A., Ormrod, J., & Bottomley, P. (2007) *Watching, Wanting and Well-being: Exploring the Links: A Study of 9-13 Year Olds.* London: National Consumer Council.

NEF (2006) *The Happy Planet Index: An Index of Human Well-being and Environmental Impact.* London: New Economics Foundation. Available at: www.happyplanetindex.org

Neisser, U. (1995) Criteria for an ecological self. In P. Rochat (Ed.) *The Self in Infancy: Theory and Research* (pp.17-34). Amsterdam, Netherlands: North-Holland/Elsevier Science Publishers.

Norgaard, K. M. (2006) "People want to protect themselves a little bit": Emotions, denial, and social movement non-participation. *Sociological Inquiry, 76*, 372-396.

Pettigrew, T. F. (1998) Intergroup contact theory. *Annual Review of Psychology, 49*, 65-85.

Plous, S. (2002) Is there such a thing as prejudice towards animals? In S. Plous (Ed.) *Understanding Prejudice and Discrimination* (pp.509-528). New York: McGraw Hill.

Porritt, J. (2005) *Capitalism as if the World Matters*, London: Earthscan.

Pratto, F., Sidanius, J., Stallworth, L.M., & Malle, B.F. (1994) Social dominance orientation: A personality variable predicting social and political attitudes. *Journal of Personality and Social Psychology, 67*, 741-764.

Reist, D.M. (2004) *Materialism vs. an Ecological Identity: Towards an Integrative Framework for a Psychology of Sustainable Living.* Unpublished doctoral dissertation.

Richins, M.L., & Dawson, S. (1992) A consumer values orientation for materialism and its measurement: Scale development and validation. *Journal of Consumer Research, 19*, 303-316.

Rokeach, M. (1973) *The Nature of Human Values.* New York: Free Press.

Rose, C., & Dade, P. (2007) Using values modes. Available at: www.campaignstrategy.org

Saucier, G. (2003) Factor structure of English-language personality type-nouns. *Journal of Personality and Social Psychology, 85*, 695-708.

Saunders, S., & Munro, D. (2000) The construction and validation of a consumer orientation questionnaire (SCOI) designed to measure Fromm's (1955) 'marketing character' in Australia. *Social Behaviour and Personality, 28*, 219-240.

Schor, J. (2004) *Born to buy: The Commercialized Child and the New Consumer Culture.* New York: Scribner.

Schwartz, S.H. (1992) Universals in the content and structure of values: Theory and empirical tests in 20 countries. In M.P. Zanna (Ed.) *Advances in Experimental Social Psychology (Vol. 25)* (pp.1-65). New York: Academic Press.

Schwartz, S.H. (2006) Basic human values: Theory, measurement, and applications. *Revue Française de Sociologie, 47*(4), 249-288.

Schultz, P.W. (2000) Empathizing with Nature: The effects of perspective taking on concern for environmental issues. *Journal of Social Issues, 56*, 391-406.

Schultz, P.W. (2001) The structure of environmental concern: Concern for self, other people, and the biosphere. *Journal of Environmental Psychology, 21*, 327-339.

Schultz, P. W. (2002). Inclusion with nature: The psychology of human-nature interactions. In P. Schmuck, & P. W. Schultz (Eds.) *The Psychology of Sustainable Development* (pp. 61-78). Boston, MA: Kluwer Academic Publishers.

Schultz, P.W., Gouveia, V.V., Cameron, L.D., Tankha, G., Schmuck, P., & Franek, M. (2005) Values and their relationship to environmental concern and conservation behaviour. *Journal of Cross-cultural Psychology, 36*, 457-475.

Seymour, L. (2003) *Nature and psychological well-being.* English Nature research reports, No.553, May 2003, English Nature, Peterborough.

Sheldon, K.M., & Kasser, T. (1995) Coherence and congruence: Two aspects of personality integration. *Journal of Personality and Social Psychology, 68*, 531-543.

Sheldon, K.M., & Kasser, T. (2008) Psychological threat and extrinsic goal striving. *Motivation and Emotion, 32*, 37-45.

Sheldon, K.M., & McGregor, H. (2000) Extrinsic value orientation and the tragedy of the commons. *Journal of Personality, 68*, 383-411.

Shellenberger, M., & Nordhaus, T. (2003) *The Death of Environmentalism: Global Warming Politics in a Post-environmental World.* The Breakthrough Institute, Oakland, CA. Available at: www.thebreakthrough.org

Solomon, S., & Arndt, J. (1993) *Cash is king: The effect of mortality salience on the appeal of money.* Unpublished data, Skidmore College.

Solomon, S., Greenberg, J., & Pyszczynski, T. (1991) A terror-management theory of social behaviour: The psychological functions of self-esteem and cultural worldviews. In M.P. Zanna (Ed.) *Advances in Experimental Social Psychology* (pp.91-159). San Diego: Academic Press.

Son Hing, L.S., Li, W., & Zanna, M.P. (2002) Inducing hypocrisy to reduce prejudicial responses among aversive racists. *Journal of Experimental Social Psychology, 38,* 71-78.

Speth, G. (2008) Environmental failure: A case for a new green politics. *Environment 360,* 20 October 2008. Available at: e360.yale.edu

Spiegel, M. (1996) *The Dreaded Comparison: Human and Animal Slavery.* New York: Mirror Books.

Stephan, W.G., & Stephan, C.W. (2000) An integrated threat theory of prejudice. In S. Oskamp (Ed.) *Reducing Prejudice and Discrimination* (pp.23-45). Mahwah, NJ: Erlbaum.

Stoll-Kleemann, S., O'Riordan, T., & Jaeger, C.C. (2001) The psychology of denial concerning climate mitigation measures: Evidence from Swiss focus groups. *Global Environmental Change, 11,* 107-117.

Sullivan, S. (2006) The Elephant in the Room? Problematising 'New' (Neoliberal) biodiversity conservation. *Forum for Development Studies, 33*(1), 105-134.

Tajfel, H., & Turner, J.C. (1986) The social identity theory of intergroup behaviour. In W.G. Austin & S. Worchel (Eds.) *Psychology of intergroup relations* (2nd Ed., pp.7-27). Chicago: Nelson-Hall.

Talberth, J., Cobb, C., & Slattery, N. (2006) *The Genuine Progress Indicator 2006: A Tool for Sustainable Development.* Redefining Progress, Oakland, US. Available at: www.rprogress.org

Thomas, K. (1983) *Man and the Natural World: Changing Attitudes in England 1500-1800.* London: Allen Lane.

Vansteenkiste, M., Simons, J., Lens, W., Sheldon, K.M., & Deci, E.L. (2004) Motivating learning, performance, and persistence. The synergistic effects of intrinsic goal contents and autonomy-supportive contexts. *Journal of Personality and Social Psychology, 87,* 246-260.

Viki, G. T., Winchester, L., Titshall, L., Chisango, T., Pina, A., & Russell, R. (2006) Beyond secondary emotions: The infrahumanization of outgroups using human-related and animal-related words. *Social Cognition, 24,* 753-775.

Vining, J. (2003) The connection to other animals and caring for nature. *Human Ecology Review, 10,* 87-99.

Warburton, D. (2008) *Evaluation of WWF-UK's Community Learning and Action for Sustainable Living (CLASL).* WWF-UK, Godalming, UK. Available at: www.wwf.org.uk

Westen, D. (2007) *The Political Brain: The Role of Emotion in Deciding the Fate of the Nation.* New York: Public Affairs.

Whitley, B.E. Jr., & Kite, M.E. (2006) *The psychology of prejudice and discrimination.* Belmont, CA: Wadsworth.

WWF (2004) *Does WWF support the hunting of the Canadian harp seal population?* 29 August, 2004. WWF-International, Gland, Switzerland.

WWF (2008) *Weathercocks and Signposts: the Environment Movement at a Cross Roads.* WWF-UK, Godalming, UK. Available at: www.wwf.org.uk/strategiesforchange

WWF (2009) *Simple and Painless? The Limitations of Spillover in Environmental Campaigning.* WWF-UK, Godalming, UK. Available at: www.wwf.org.uk/strategiesforchange

WWF (in press) *The Natural Change Project: Working with the Psychology of Sustainability.* WWF Scotland, Dunkeld, UK. Available at: www.naturalchange.org.uk

Zavestoski, S. (2003) Constructing and maintaining ecological identities: The strategies of deep ecology. In S. Clayton & S. Opotow (Eds.) *Identity and the natural environment* (pp.297-315). Cambridge, MA: MIT Press.

Zeidner, M., & Endler, N.S. (Eds.) (1996) *Handbook of Coping: Theory, Research, Applications.* New York: John Wiley & Sons.

About the authors

Tom Crompton is Change Strategist at WWF-UK, Godalming, Surrey, UK, where he has developed WWF's Strategies for Change Project. He is author of the WWF-UK report *Weathercocks and Signposts: The Environment Movement at a Crossroads* and co-author of *Simple and Painless? The Limitations of Spillover in Environmental Campaigning*. He holds a PhD in evolutionary biology from the University of Leicester, and a BA in natural sciences from the University of Cambridge, UK. He can be contacted at: tcrompton@wwf.org.uk

Tim Kasser is Professor of Psychology at Knox College, in Galesburg, Illinois, USA, where he teaches classes on personality, clinical and abnormal psychology, and alternatives to consumerism. He has published dozens of scientific articles and book chapters on how people's values and goals relate to their quality of life and their social and environmental behaviour. Kasser is also the author of *The High Price of Materialism* (MIT Press, 2002) and co-editor of *Psychology and Consumer Culture* (APA, 2004). He holds a PhD in psychology from the University of Rochester, New York, and a BA in psychology from Vanderbilt University, Tennessee. He can be contacted at: tkasser@knox.edu

Acknowledgements

The authors are grateful to the following individuals for their help or their comments on earlier drafts of this paper: Joe Brewer, Niamh Carey, Julia Crompton, Patrick Curry, Deborah Du Nann Winter, Alun Evans, Stephen Fitzpatrick, Jamie Goldenberg, Oliver Greenfield, Liz Jackson, Tim Jackson, Allen Kanner, Virginia Kasser, David Key, Melissa Lane, Renée Lertzman, Peter Lipman, Mike Maniates, Alastair McIntosh, Mike Morris, Ciaran Mundy, David Norman, Jules Peck, Katie Randerson, Wesley Schultz, Kelly Shaw, Sian Sullivan, and Jules Weston.